CW00971963

TRANSFORMATIVE

LEADERSHIP

TRANSFORMATIVE

LEADERSHIP

Developing the Hidden Dimension

Eloy Anello

Joan Hernandez

May Khadem

TRANSFORMATIVE LEADERSHIP
Copyright 2014 © by Eloy Anello, Joan Hernandez, May Khadem

Published by Harmony Equity Press
Houston, TX
HarmonyEquity.com

All Rights Reserved

No part of this book may be reproduced or transmitted in any form by any means: graphic, electronic, or mechanical, including photocopying, recording, taping or by any information storage or retrieval system without permission, in writing, from the authors, except for the inclusion of brief quotations in a review, article, book, or academic paper. The authors and publisher of this book and the associated materials have used their best efforts in preparing this material. The authors and publisher make no representations or warranties with respect to accuracy, applicability, fitness or completeness of the contents of this material. They disclaim any warranties expressed or implied, merchantability, or fitness for any particular purpose. The authors and publisher shall in no event be held liable for any loss or other damages, including but not limited to special, incidental, consequential, or other damages. If you have any questions or concerns, the advice of a competent professional should be sought.

Manufactured in the United States of America.

ISBN: 978-1-941431-00-9

Library of Congress Control Number: 2014938936

We humbly dedicate this book to Dr. Rahmatullah Muhájir, who provided a living example of transformative leadership for all who came in contact with him, and inspired our understanding of the essential elements of true leadership.

Contents

PART I
TRANSFORMATION OF UNDERSTANDING

PART II
DEVELOPING CAPABILITIES

PREFACE

The approach to leadership presented in this book evolved over several decades. Dr. Eloy Anello first began wrestling with ideas related to leadership while working in public health in Bolivia in the 1970s, when he realized that it was impossible to get community organizations to function properly without strengthening the leadership capabilities of their members. He also recognized that prevailing modes of top-down leadership were disempowering to community organizations. In his search for alternative modes of leadership, he was inspired by 'Abdu'l-Bahá's description in *The Secret of Divine Civilization* of the role of the learned as the leaven of society and of the four conditions of a learned person.[1] Thus, he began to understand the importance of personal transformation, self-discipline, obedience to truth, and education based on comprehensive knowledge as essential elements of leadership.

In 1988 the World Health Organization first used the term *moral leadership* to refer to the type of leadership that was needed at all levels of society to meet its goals of *Health for All by the Year 2000*. Before then, the moral dimension of leadership tended to be ignored in the discourse on social and economic development. The use of this term by a prominent international organization marked the first step in a growing openness to including moral and spiritual issues in the discourse on development, and the term was adopted to describe the model of leadership that Dr. Anello and his colleagues at Núr University were slowly beginning to elaborate.

With the opening up of the Soviet Union, the need for an alternative framework for moral education became increasingly apparent to educators in that country. The work of Dr. Farzam Arbab at the Rural University in Colombia, with its focus on development of capabilities and integration of moral issues with academic topics, caught the attention of Herzen University in St. Petersburg, Russia. In 1992 this university invited a number of educators from different parts of the world, including Dr. Arbab and Dr. Anello, to meet in St. Petersburg, where their thinking coalesced in the formulation of 4 elements of the conceptual framework and 15 capabilities of moral leadership.

Upon returning to Bolivia, Dr. Anello began incorporating these ideas of moral leadership in the seminars and workshops on "Community Leadership" that he was giving to non-governmental organizations under the auspices of Nur University. But he had a special love for rural schoolteachers, whom he perceived to be key underutilized human resources. Finally, his dream of offering training in community development to rural schoolteachers was realized when Nur University obtained funding to launch a 3-semester pilot project to give them specialized training in this field. The philosophical underpinning of the course was the conceptual framework and the capabilities of moral leadership. Joan Barstow Hernandez, who at that time was directing the literacy program at Nur University and had already written several books,[2] was designated as coordinator of the project.

Working together, Dr. Anello and Ms. Hernandez developed a 12-module course. The positive response of the 500 schoolteachers who initially took the course was so encouraging that it led to the development of a number of other related materials. The 3-semester program has been replicated, not only in Bolivia, but also in Ecuador with 1000 participants, in Argentina with 300 participants, and on a smaller scale in other Latin American and Caribbean countries. Moreover, numerous workshops on moral leadership and the capabilities of moral leadership, varying in length from 3 to 15 days, have been given throughout the world: in Latin America, North America, Europe, Africa and Asia.

Based on successive training experiences, the module on *Moral Leadership* was refined and amplified to incorporate new learning. It was also translated into English in the form of a training manual to facilitate its use in countries around the world.

Meanwhile, Dr. May Khadem, co-founder and Executive Director of Health for Humanity, a non-profit health development organization, had become aware of the need to incorporate an ethical component in its training programs. An evaluation of one of its long term projects revealed that technical training, the primary focus of the organization up to that point, had created well-trained human resources and a better standard of health care in the projects it had been involved with. However, the poor and those in greatest need still did not have access to that care.

Dr. Khadem requested assistance from Dr. Anello to help incorporate Nur's leadership training into its health development initiatives. Nur-trained facilitators assisted Health for Humanity to develop the capacity to incorporate the leadership training program alongside its technical training. Over the course of 6 years, moral leadership training was adapted for the health sector and the manual was translated into various languages. Leadership training thus became an integral part of Health for Humanity training, particularly in the work of blindness prevention. It was well received everywhere and provided the missing ethical framework to guide the newly acquired technical skills of doctors. The combination of an evidence-based medical practice within the guidelines of an ethical framework provided the clarity needed for institutional and individual development and decision-making.

In 2008 and 2009 Dr. Khadem worked with Dr. Anello to offer elements of this training to representatives of ministries of health in the World Health Organization's *Good Governance in Medicines Programme*. During this period, under the auspices of SecondMuse, the manual was updated and re-written for health professionals.

Prior to his passing, Dr. Anello expressed interest in producing a book that would capture and expand upon the essence and learning that he and Ms. Hernandez had developed over the years related to moral leadership, enriched by the work that he had done with Dr. Khadem. He wished to make it available to both individuals and institutions as they struggled to address the challenges in their personal lives and in the institutions they served. In 2008, he invited Dr. Khadem to go to Bolivia and work with him and Ms. Hernandez to accomplish this. Unfortunately, Dr. Anello's state of health did not permit this. However, honoring his wish, since his passing, Ms. Hernandez and Dr. Khadem have worked together to produce this book in English. It's title, *Transformative Leadership: Developing the Hidden Dimension,* underscores the importance of transformation as a purpose of leadership. Furthermore, it acknowledges the critical importance of developing those inner qualities and values upon which the visible skills of leadership rest.

ACKNOWLEDGEMENTS

We are grateful to so many who have contributed in numerous ways to make this book possible and without whose input it could not have materialized.

First, we extend our heartfelt thanks to Dr. Farzam Arbab, Mr. Paul Lample, Ms. Lori McLaughlin Nogouchi, and the other participants of the International Moral Education team that met at Hertzen Pedagogical University in St. Petersburg, Russia in 1992, where they identified 15 of the moral leadership capabilities and laid the groundwork for the conceptual framework described in this book.

We express our deepest appreciation to colleagues at Nur University. Without their shared vision of the role that a university can play in the process of personal and social transformation and their commitment to programs that contribute to this end, neither the book nor the many programs that have developed from it would have come into existence.

Further appreciation goes to the hundreds of Bolivian schoolteachers, participants in the first program of "Community Development founded on Moral Leadership," who awakened us to the powerful transformational effect that the concepts of moral leadership can have on those who study them and make a sincere effort to put them into practice. We are also grateful to the thousands of participants in different parts of the world, whose questions, comments and suggestions have helped to enrich our own understanding of transformative leadership and to more fully develop many of the ideas included in this book.

In writing this book, we express deep appreciation to Peter Newton, one of the trainers in the program of Educational Leadership in Ecuador, who contributed generously to the research and writing of the chapter on "Mental Models of Human Nature and Society."

We are also grateful to Mr. John Kepner and Mr. Charles Howard who were instrumental in helping Health for Humanity develop the capacity to adapt and incorporate the leadership training program for its health projects.

Special thanks goes to the Social Investment Fund of Bolivia and Plan International for sponsoring the writing of the initial versions of the manual in Spanish, to USAID for sponsoring the program with one thousand teachers in Ecuador, to SecondMuse (secondmuse.com) for the opportunity to rewrite the manual for health professionals, to Guitelle Sabeti for the invitation to offer the training to representatives of Ministries of Health in WHO's Good Governance in Medicines Programme, and to Jeff Parker and the Vision in Practice team in China for incorporating the material into training for ophthalmologists and eye hospital personnel.

Finally, our immense gratitude to Mozhan Khadem for his critical review of the manuscript, to Richard Czerniejewski for his editorial assistance and to Arya Badiyan for cover design, editorial assistance, and completing the final phase of publication and distribution.

TRIBUTE TO DR. ELOY ANELLO (1946-2009)

Eloy,… left the United States and settled in Bolivia in the early 1970s, making it his home and dedicating himself to the upliftment of its people. No one who crossed his path could fail to be touched by his unbounded energy, by his sincere love of humanity, which he brought to every enterprise he undertook.… How many young people were awakened to the crying needs of humanity as a result of his efforts.… How many were galvanized to arise and serve.… So dedicated was he to nurturing young minds that he co-founded Universidad Nur in Santa Cruz (Bolivia) — an institution striving … for the advancement of the indigenous populations.[3]

I wish to take this opportunity to express my gratitude to Eloy for all that he meant in my life. Working closely with him during 1993 and 1994 to produce the 12 modules for the program, "Moral Leadership for Agents of Community Development," and facilitating workshops together in that program transformed my life professionally. At times I felt as if I were in an individualized post-graduate program, in which I read, broadened my ideas through enriching dialogues with Eloy, wrote, presented my writing for his review, and then shared the results with the participants through workshops.

Furthermore, Eloy's humble and egalitarian attitude deeply impressed me. When we began to give workshops together, in spite of the fact that he had decades of experience and I had much less, he always treated me as an equal. It was truly an example of 'assisted empowerment' quickly leading to 'mutual empowerment.'

Some years later, in the closing ceremony of the extremely successful program of Educational Leadership in Ecuador, I could not attend for family reasons. Friends later informed me that when the participants praised and thanked Eloy for the program, he responded, "I didn't prepare the modules by myself. There is a co-author, who is not with us today." There was a possibility that I might never hear of this comment, but the naturalness with which he shared the recognition that he was receiving is just one example of the way in which Eloy exemplified service-oriented leadership in his own life.

Joan Barstow Hernández

One of the great gifts of my life was the opportunity to work with Eloy Anello and to experience first hand his transformative leadership. His encouragement, his confidence in the capacity of those around him, his collaborative style, his absolute faith in the power of consultation, his firm adherence to justice and unity, combined with his genuine warmth and humility have made him, for me, a powerful role model. I have been privileged to participate in the writing of this book upon Eloy's instruction. I hope that he would find the work I have done, with his inspiration, acceptable both in quality and in spirit.

May Khadem

INTRODUCTION

The world is calling for a new model of leadership that effectively addresses today's challenges. Formulas, gimmicks and easy answers have proven their bankruptcy. The only enduring summons that rings true from our recent past are the words of Mahatma Gandhi, *"Be the change you wish to see in the world."* But how do we do that? The purpose of this book is to help individuals and organizations to *be* that change – to adopt leadership styles that are transformative, both for individuals and for the institutions and societies in which they participate.

There is a logical progression to the chapters based on the latest thinking in adult learning. The contents are best assimilated in an interactive learning environment such as a workshop, where participants collaborate to enhance each other's understanding. But the book can also serve as a personal manual for self-improvement.

The chapters guide the readers through a profound learning process that can change their lives. Unlike most kinds of learning, our aim is not to provide more information or novel ideas. Our aim is to change the way people think. Insight into the adult learning process, especially the kind that we are employing in transformative leadership training, will help us to understand the essential steps, identified through research, that we must traverse if this kind of life-changing learning is to take place.

Unlike children, adults come to educational activities with a rich history of prior learning. Their cultural background and experiences have combined to create their own unique worldviews. Different authors use different names to refer to the ways in which we see the world. Worldview, frame of reference, mind set, habits of mind, paradigms, and mental models all refer to generally the same thing – a set of automatically adopted assumptions about the world and how it works. Usually these are unconscious and we don't even realize that they exist. However, they color everything we see and interact with. Mental models are inevitable and help us order our world and make sense out of it. They can be helpful, harmful, or neutral.

There are two kinds of learning we engage in: *in*formative and *trans*formative. Most learning is informative. We add facts, ideas, and concepts to our fund of knowledge. The new information adds depth and breadth to our ways of looking at the world, but it does not change how we look at the world. It might change the *content* of our thinking, but not the *structure* of our thinking. We generally file new information into our current mental models. If it complies with our mental model, we accept the information as true. If the information challenges our mental model, we generally assume the information to be false and disregard it. Alternatively, we might rationalize and file it away as an anomaly.

Informative learning is critical to our becoming masters in our professions; it gives us the detailed, in-depth knowledge necessary to carry out highly skilled work with expertise. For example, it is easy to understand why surgeons, airplane pilots, engineers, architects, or other highly skilled professionals requiring precise technical knowledge and expertise need very sophisticated depth of information and skill to carry out their work.

The approach to transformative leadership, however, requires a different kind of learning called *transformative* learning. This term was coined in the 1970's by Jack Mezirow[1] who was studying the learning of women returning to higher education and the workforce after a hiatus of some years, who not only had to acquire new information, but also new ways of thinking in order to succeed. Transformative learning challenges our ways of thinking and helps us to critically examine the fundamental assumptions underlying our worldview or mental models, resulting in life-changing insights.

This kind of learning goes beyond the accumulation of facts and information; it challenges us to update our behavior to conform to new understandings of reality. We can no longer hang new information into our past frames of reference. Transformative learning requires that we become aware of our own unexamined assumptions and those of others and expose them to analysis and scrutiny so that we can objectively see their contribution to the truth of a situation. And, if required, we must change our frame of reference, or mental model, to conform to new information. This represents a fundamental shift in the way we think.

A clear appreciation of this process is critical to taking charge of our own learning in a socially responsible way and helping others to do the same. Once we have deconstructed mental models that are found limiting, we are in a position to construct new *conceptual frameworks* more consistent with reality. Transformative learning helps us to "own" our values, feelings, beliefs, and thinking instead of automatically assimilating them from others. Its hallmark is an independent and unfettered search for truth and the recognition that it is our moral responsibility to be committed to such a process.

Educators describe a specific process that is required for transformative learning to occur. The first four steps listed below are adapted from the work of Jack Mezirow. They have to do with opening ourselves to change. The final two steps are newer additions to the process gleaned from other researchers in the field and our own experience. This 6-step process includes: *providing context, challenging mental models, transforming our understanding through critical analysis, adopting a new conceptual framework, participating in a learning community* and *taking action.* We have expanded on this critical last step – *taking action* – by elaborating 18 capabilities that give us the tools we need to translate our new understandings into action.

As we review these steps, we will relate them to the content in the corresponding chapters in the book.

▶ PROVIDING CONTEXT

Understanding context is critical to all adult learning, but it is indispensable for transformative learning. All that we know and believe, including our values and feelings, depend on our particular historical and cultural context. All our unexamined assumptions have been adopted unconsciously from our unique set of experiences. Transformative learning involves exposing those automatically adopted beliefs to the light of scrutiny using larger and more inclusive historical and inter-cultural contexts. Without context we cannot determine the truth of our understanding. When a more inclusive and broader context with rational appeal informs our understanding, we are more willing to release our prior limiting points of view. Examining our particular challenge in the light of our past history, our present situation, and our desired future provides context. It helps us understand how we came to adopt our particular ways of looking at the world, how these impact our challenges, and how they might limit what we hope to achieve. It helps us, in a way, to "step outside of ourselves," so that we can look at a larger picture. Examining our historical perspective is central to appreciating the need for critical analysis of unexamined mental models.

In order to provide this context, we begin Chapter I with an analysis of the "Crisis of Our Times." This examines the twin processes of integration and disintegration that characterize our age and puts them into the larger context of the collective social development of humanity. It tries to create a coherent historical perspective for the seemingly random and senseless crises that surround us.

While we appreciate that many of our trusted institutions are seriously flawed, we recognize that there are new institutions and systems that are emerging to support our new collective interdependence. This helps us to understand the seemingly contradictory forces at work in the world and how to make sense out of what may, at first glance, appear to be random and confusing events.

Finally, the chapter identifies the lack of moral leadership at all levels of society as our greatest challenge in addressing the numerous global crises before us. We come to understand that the lack of ethical leadership is but one of the myriad manifestations of the general breakdown in moral values found in society. Examining our current "learning moment" in history puts our ethical challenges into a framework of growth and development. It relates our current condition to our past history and sheds light on an emerging healthier future.

▶ CHALLENGING MENTAL MODELS

Critical to the process of transformative learning is becoming aware of our own and others' tacit assumptions and expectations. These are what we unconsciously assume to be true, what is taken for granted, what we might call "conventional wisdom." When these unexamined assumptions cluster together, they result in automatic responses which Mezirow calls "habits of mind" that together give us a particular frame of reference that we mistakenly assume to be *the truth*. They become our *mental models,* our unique points of view through which we interpret all experience. They then dictate whether we will approach an issue from a conservative or liberal orientation, whether we approach others with openness or suspicion, if we are fearful or trusting, etc. They are lenses through which we view the world, filter what we see and how we see it, and determine an automatic course of action that we will follow.

Transformative learning demands that we recognize that we all hold these unexamined assumptions and mental models that color how we view the world and that unless we scrutinize them critically and unemotionally with the goal of finding the flaws in our thinking, we cannot make the learning leap to a new and more profound level of understanding.

Of course, not all mental models are bad. Mental models are necessary for us to navigate our way in the world and help us to create order and context for our experiences. Some are consistent with truth and very useful; some are neutral and are neither helpful nor harmful. Others, however, are limiting and prevent us from achieving our true potential. For example, there are mental models that relate to gender and race that may cause us to discriminate against other people because of our prejudices. It is these dysfunctional mental models that we wish to expose to scrutiny so that we may free ourselves from their constraining influence and become able to adopt new understandings more consistent with truth.

Understanding mental models is particularly important when we seek solutions to difficult problems. The way we think about the problem and the solutions we seek have to be creative, bold and aligned with truth. When we are charting a new path, this becomes especially critical, as we need to see clearly and make our decisions with conscious awareness. Dysfunctional mental models about human nature, society and leadership are impediments that prevent us from developing the type of leadership that today's world demands. They need to be scrutinized and replaced with *conceptual frameworks* that are more coherent with reality.

▶ TRANSFORMING UNDERSTANDING

Engaging in the process of transformative learning is not easy. Human beings develop in a social context. Our awareness and understanding of the world and everything about it is essentially based on relationships with others. Our identities are developed within webs of social interaction and shared cultural life. All that we experience, including our history and our language, and the very manner in which we express our most profound thoughts and feelings are deeply embedded in our cultural heritage. Stepping outside that context and questioning the most fundamental assumptions is no easy task and may, indeed, trigger a profoundly disturbing emotional upheaval or existential crisis.

Challenging our cherished beliefs is a leap into the unknown and can be threatening, even frightening. We rarely choose to go down this unsettling path without provocation. It is when we encounter problems and challenges that defy our "habits of mind" that we are forced to re-examine fundamental assumptions. It is usually during a time of crisis, when what we are doing no longer works, that we are forced to find new pathways. We are, indeed, now *collectively* living through such a time of crisis in human history.

The most fundamental assumptions about who we are individually and collectively, the institutions and the societies we have established, and the manner in which we relate to each other and the planet, are now all under scrutiny. As disturbing as this is, it is also a stage set for transformation. Transformative learning is often initiated by *crisis.* Generally, we become critically reflective of those beliefs that become problematic, what Mezirow refers to as, "disorienting dilemmas." Since what we know no longer works, we are forced to examine unknown territory. This requires not only courage, but also creativity and imagination. We have to be able to examine alternative interpretations of experience by "trying on" other points of view and seeing how they fit. We transform our points of view by becoming critically reflective of the content and/or process of solving the problem and challenging the underlying assumptions. As we engage in this process, we become acutely aware of those assumptions that we have held all our lives that are flawed. It is like taking a dirty mirror and polishing it so that we can see the true reflection of reality. No matter how attached we might be to our previously held assumptions, once we see their flaws, we can no longer look at the world in the same way. This is the transformation of understanding in the light of truth.

In Chapters II and III, we begin the process of challenging mental models and transforming our understanding in three interrelated areas that concern us in this book: human nature, society and leadership.

In Chapter II, "Mental Models of Human Nature and Society," we expose several pseudo-scientific theories of human nature and social order as dysfunctional mental models. We challenge their legitimacy in justifying aggression, selfishness, conflict and competition as "natural" and "immutable" characteristics of human beings and society. We expose the faulty assumptions upon which these models are based and present compelling evidence that indicates that mutuality and co-operation are the distinctive characteristics of human beings, guiding the reader to a transformation of understanding.

In Chapter III, we examine "Dominant Models of Leadership," identifying the distinguishing traits of four mental models of leadership: authoritarian, paternalistic, know-it-all, and manipulative. We see the dysfunctional effect of each model and how each concentrates power in the hands of the leader. We also analyze democratic leadership in terms of its limitations as it is currently practiced in the world. The outcome of this analysis leaves us with the unsettling, even disturbing, realization that there is no model of leadership widely practiced in the world that provides the guidance we need to address the immense problems confronting humanity. We come to recognize that this period of crisis is, indeed, our opportunity for transformation.

▶ ADOPTING A NEW CONCEPTUAL FRAMEWORK

Once we understand the limitations of our mental models, we are in a much better position to construct or adopt a new *conceptual framework* based on principles and values upon which we agree. The purpose of *group consultation*, or what Mezirow calls "reflective discourse," is to search for common understanding, to see the broader perspective and a more inclusive viewpoint. It is our best tool for accessing the larger truth.

There are generally three sources of knowledge that we can tap into for constructing a new conceptual framework: scientific evidence, universally recognized ethical principles, and experience. We need to examine all available facts and evidence, interpret available information from multiple angles, evaluate that information informed by ethical principles, reflect on our individual and collective experiences, and arrive at the most rational understanding given the particular set of circumstances. When we explore the evidence in the light of our particular experience, we have to realize that unlike the prevailing approach to issues in many cultures, there are more than two sides to an issue. In fact, the more sides we examine, the more informed we would be. We have to transcend our cultural proclivity for "seeing two, and only two, sides" (as in debate), seeing everything as a contest between two opposing parties, or settling differences by litigation. In fact, we have to be open to all possibilities.

Effectively engaging in group consultation requires new capabilities and skills that have to be learned and nurtured. These include trust, solidarity and empathy, among others. We need to learn how to listen actively, collaborate, exercise courtesy, adopt a stance of humility, and withhold judgment. Most importantly, we must focus the light of moral values on whatever we assume to be true and ensure that it passes the test of ethics. Leadership, a mental model that typically connotes being a "commander," is then transformed into a new model of "service to the common good."

In Chapter IV, "Elements of the Conceptual Framework of Transformative Leadership," we offer a new framework for consideration, consisting of six elements: *service-oriented leadership, personal and social transformation, investigation and application of truth, essential nobility of human beings, transcendence,* and *development of leadership capabilities.*

The elements of this framework are based on universal ethical principles and consistent with what we know from current thinking in the social sciences. All cultures of the world share a fundamental spiritual core that gives rise to moral values and ethical principles that are absolute and not relative in terms of time and place. The values of truthfulness, justice, integrity, honesty, compassion, kindness, generosity, courtesy, etc., are not unique to any particular society, but are embraced by all and are deeply rooted in all cultures. Therefore, the conceptual framework that we propose is applicable across all societies. All people everywhere will find resonance with what is already within their own core values. It is precisely this — *our collective spiritual heritage* — that unites us into one global community and one family.

▶ FORMING A LEARNING COMMUNITY

Embracing a new conceptual framework is, of course, not enough. Real transformation is manifested in changed behavior. But translating new insights into new behaviors and measurable outcomes is not easy. And doing so all alone is especially daunting. Because of this, being part of a like-minded community with the same vision and desire for change is vitally important for three reasons: such a community provides invaluable support, escalates the pace of learning, and has greater impact on society.

There is extraordinary power in the reinforcing relationships within a community that nurtures a new conceptual framework as it is taking hold. Such a small group of people can nurture and apply new transformative ideas until a time when the transformation reaches a critical mass that catalyzes change in the larger institution or society. We explore these ideas in greater depth in Chapter IV when we expound on the concept of transformation.

While much of the book focuses on critically analyzing mental models and adopting a new conceptual framework, we must not lose sight of our aim — our purpose is not just our own personal transformation, but *collective* transformation. Transformative learning not only can, but *must* also occur, at a *collective* level, if we are to successfully address the challenges before us.

In adult education, the process of transformative learning in a group or organizational setting is called "collaborative inquiry." This refers to the process, in a group setting, of highly participatory activities that are designed to enhance learning from experience through repeated cycles of action and reflection on that action. We refer to this process as "group consultation" using the "learning cycle" as explored in depth in Part II, where we elaborate on the capabilities needed for transformative leadership.

▶ TRANSLATING NEW UNDERSTANDING INTO ACTION

As we have already noted, it is not enough to expand our awareness, adopt more inclusive understanding, and have a more profound grasp of what is true and real. If this is not manifested in action, we have only engaged in interesting intellectual exercises with no lasting results. True transformation impels us to action, for a truly expanded understanding requires that we conform how we act to what we know. Otherwise, we are guilty of hypocrisy.

What is required is not only the will to change, but also the power to act. Transformation implies not just *seeing* life from a new vantage point, but *living* life from that new perspective. Taking action based on our expanded understanding leads to new experiences. These new experiences then require further critical reflection that provides new insights and meaning. We need tools to assist us to change and to manifest that change in our behaviors, both individually and collectively. In Part II, we elaborate on 18 capabilities that we need to translate our new understanding into change that will result in both our own individual as well as our collective transformation. These capabilities are divided into four categories: capabilities that contribute to personal transformation, capabilities that contribute to better interpersonal relationships, capabilities that contribute to social transformation, and one integrative capability focused on the process of learning to apply all the capabilities.

In the Epilogue, we conclude with, "A Word About Ambition," an analysis of some ways in which self-centered ambition can poison the whole process, distorting transformative leadership. Of course, ambition to love and serve others contributes to the well-being of all and to a better world. But we must be vigilant and guard against the destructive effects of egotistical tendencies. Therefore, we offer some thoughts on qualities that can protect us from the pernicious influence of unbridled ambition.

PART I

TRANSFORMATION

OF

UNDERSTANDING

CHAPTER I

THE CRISIS OF OUR TIMES

The lesson of history is that to the degree people and civilizations have operated in harmony with correct principles, they have prospered. At the root of societal declines are foolish practices that represent violations of correct principles.[1]

– Stephen Covey

AN OVERVIEW OF OUR AGE

We live in an age in which the world has witnessed dramatic changes that have profoundly altered the nature of society and submerged it in a state of unprecedented anxiety and confusion — an age in which we can behold the rapid disintegration of the structures of civilization itself. It is not hard to find ample examples of crises in our world. Just open the newspaper on any given day. The crises are so many and so varied that it is difficult not to feel pessimistic and cynical. Not only do we see the overwhelming problems before us, but also they all seem to be coalescing, reinforcing each other and magnifying their damaging effects.

A crisis in one global system would be bad enough, but there are so many reaching a peak simultaneously — the escalation of natural disasters attributed to global warming and environmental destruction; the corrosive effects of greed and dishonesty on the financial underpinnings of the global financial systems; the failed ideologies of both communism and unbridled capitalism; the cancerous growth of materialism extending its reach into the remotest areas of the world and threatening to choke off the viability of cultural traditions and ways of life; the breakdown of healthy human relationships with the attendant consequences of gangs, abuse of women and children, indiscriminant violence, and the rampage of terror.

However, not everything is negative. This age can be compared to a tapestry where strands of light and darkness, of promise and despair are tightly interwoven. No one would dispute the tremendous challenges we face in the world, but signs of hope can also be discerned.

With the simultaneous development of communications at the speed of light and transportation at the speed of sound, the world has contracted into a mere neighborhood in which people are instantly aware of one another's affairs and have immediate access to one another. And yet, even with such miraculous advances, with the emergence of international organizations, and with valiant attempts and brilliant successes at international cooperation, nations are at woeful odds with one another, people are convulsed by economic upheavals, minorities feel more alienated than ever and are filled with mistrust, humiliation and fear.

Collateral with these changes has been the breakdown of institutions, religious and political, which traditionally functioned as the guideposts for the stability of society. Even the most resilient of these seem to be losing their credibility as they have become preoccupied with their own internal disorder. This calls attention to the emptiness of the moral landscape and the feeling of futility deranging personal life…

Disunity is the crux of the problems that so severely afflict the planet. It permeates attitudes in all departments of life. It is at the heart of all major conflicts between nations and peoples…[2]

Disunity is related to the decline in morality. When human beings forget their commitment to moral principles a disintegrative process begins in which "the nerves of discipline are relaxed, the voice of human conscience is stilled, the sense of decency and shame is obscured, conceptions of duty, of solidarity, of reciprocity, and of loyalty are distorted and the very feeling of peacefulness, of joy and of hope is gradually extinguished."[3] Evidence of this can be seen at all levels of society, especially in the ethical malaise and corruption among officials both in public and private institutions.

Without a commitment to moral principles, it is all too easy to ignore the common good when it interferes with individual profit. Justice then goes by the wayside. Without justice, true unity is impossible. Without both justice and unity, it is impossible to implement enduring solutions to problems, whether they are large or small.

What are some of these universal ethical values to which we need to pay more attention? Many of them are articulated in different declarations of the United Nations, especially *The Universal Declaration of Human Rights*. The most fundamental of these shared values are found within the cultural and spiritual heritage of people the world over. They have to do with honesty, integrity, uprightness, justice, fair-mindedness, truthfulness, and trustworthiness.

It is the flagrant disregard for these values that leads to corruption, and even more ominously, to the breakdown of the foundations of time honored institutions and current systems of order that were previously considered inviolable – systems that had lulled us into a false feeling of security until the mounting pace of upheavals unveiled the underlying global malaise. The world financial systems, governance, the environment, and even the very food we eat – to name only a few – are all suffering decline. With accelerating rapidity we see the shifting footholds that only recently seemed secure.

A PARADIGM SHIFT

This shock between a yesterday which is losing relevance but still seeking to survive, and a tomorrow which is gaining substance, characterizes the phase of transition as a time of announcement and a time of decision.[4]

– *Paolo Freire*

What causes such rampant disregard for the values that people everywhere have accepted and honored? The answer, in part, has to do with the fact that we are living at a time that requires a paradigm shift. The ways in which we are accustomed to seeing society and ourselves are not coherent with a world that has shrunk to a neighborhood. Our assumptions about 'the way things are' originate in childhood and adolescence. They are based on the understanding of reality that prevails within our cultural context and, for the most part, are adopted without analysis or questioning. When enough people hold the same limited views of reality, we are inclined to passively accept them as truth even when evidence indicates otherwise. Because these views are so widely accepted, the majority assumes that they accurately represent reality and few see a need to examine them critically and expose their flaws.

In his seminal book on organizational development, *The Fifth Discipline*, Peter Senge reflects on this phenomenon and refers to unexamined assumptions of this kind as *mental models*.[5] The influential scientist-philosopher, Thomas Kuhn, refers to the worldview that underlies interrelated mental models as a *paradigm*.[6] These are ways of looking at the world based on our limited understanding. They are useful to the extent that they offer a social context and frame our understanding, but they also can become rigid filters through which we view the world, only allowing us to process certain information. When information presents itself that does not conform to the mental model, we either do not notice it or reject it out of hand without any attempt to test or analyze its truth or validity. A good example of a rigid worldview that resisted truth was the Ptolemaic concept of the earth as the center of the universe. Copernicus challenged this view, and Galileo further elaborated the new understanding when he proposed that, in fact, the sun, not the earth, is the center. This concept was so radical and threatening to the prevailing worldview that Galileo spent the last years of his life under house arrest.

The shift from an outdated or dysfunctional worldview that no longer serves the purpose of truth and progress, to one that is more aligned with new evidence and is more holistic is what Kuhn calls a *paradigm shift*. The process of aligning with a more comprehensive understanding of reality requires that we examine the ways in which we view the world and the assumptions upon which these are based and expose them to critical scrutiny. We need to identify our mental models, critically analyze them, subject them to scientific evidence and discard them if they are not accurate representations of what we know to be true.

However, we need to be careful that the yardstick we use to determine the truth or falsity of our worldview does not rest on unverified assumptions of its own. Sometimes, even in the name of science, we dismiss the truth without careful scrutiny. Biologist Rupert Sheldrake asserts that the current materialistic approach of science is founded upon many assumptions that are unproven. These include: everything is mechanical, there is no purpose or direction to life or evolution, all inheritance is material, memories are stored as material traces, minds are confined to brains, etc. Many of these assertions are not based on evidence and are, one by one, being challenged by modern insights.[7]

The process of critical scrutiny of our assumptions is not easy and may evoke an existential crisis for those whose lives are built on the foundation of mental models that are found to be false. However, in the long run, if the foundation is untrue, sooner or later the structure will collapse. This is what we are witnessing with the break down of so many institutions in our society that only a few years ago seemed impervious to change.

In order to align ourselves with a worldview that is more coherent with reality, we have to acknowledge that, like the authorities who condemned Galileo and clung to outdated worldviews, perhaps we, too, are operating within an illusory paradigm that has become outdated and dysfunctional. We, too, have to apply the rigors of true scientific inquiry to the most fundamental assumptions we make about who we are and the foundations upon which we construct our societies.

The corruption and conflict that we witness around us are only manifestations of an endemic problem that affects all the structures of society, including the way we live our individual lives. If, indeed, the problem is endemic and so entrenched, we might reasonably ask, "Is there any hope of changing it?" Like Galileo, who could not foresee the far-reaching results of his fidelity to truth, we are obliged to carefully and critically examine the evidence and raise awareness, with confidence that the paradigm is, indeed, already shifting.

An important element of this new emerging paradigm is the recognition of the inter-relationship and interconnection of all of life. Developments in science from quantum physics to astrophysics, from biology to ecology to sociology, all support the new paradigm, providing evidence that everything is connected and interrelated. Advances in nuclear physics have proven that events at the subatomic level can have instantaneous impact on events far removed in space from the originating event, a phenomenon called "non-locality." In 1964, John Stewart Bell demonstrated that when paired subatomic particles are separated even by great distances, a change in one can instantaneously affect its mate, a puzzling kind of communication, even faster than the speed of light, now referred to as Bell's Theorem.[8]

When we view the macroscopic aspects of life, we see similar evidence of interconnection. There is increasing consensus among climatologists that the accelerating frequency of weather extremes and natural disasters can be directly linked to global warming.[9] There is now compelling evidence that human activity has resulted in greenhouse gases that contribute to increasing the planet's temperature with the consequent changes in the earth's atmosphere and in meteorological phenomena. How we live our lives has a macroscopic impact that affects the planet itself.

Similarly, in biology we see new insights about the interconnection of all life. According to Gaia theory, first proposed by biologist James

Lovelock, the earth is a complex and self-regulating system, embracing all of life including the sum total of soil, water, air, and organisms. It is a living, evolving and highly interdependent whole. Changes, large or small, in any part, affect the entirety.[10] When first proposed in the 1970s, the Gaia hypothesis met strong opposition and even faced ridicule from the scientific community. However, in his seminal paper published in *Nature* in 1990, Lovelock provided ample scientific evidence for Gaia theory, thereby gaining increasing support from the mainstream scientific community.[11]

Over the past few decades, this new understanding has continued gaining support from a wide variety of disciplines within the basic sciences as well as the social sciences, leading a number of thinkers to draw implications for humanity's collective social evolution. Evolutionary biologist Elisabet Sahtouris proposes: "A conscious, self-creating living cosmos is one in which life is sacred, ethics are inherent in evolutionary maturation processes and humanity itself can follow countless other species out of a juvenile mode of competitive aggression and into mature cooperation, a process I believe is apparent in our struggle to move beyond win/lose oil economics and into the establishment of true global family."[12]

These scientific advances show us that fragmentation is an illusion. Yet our cultures and life styles are based on a fragmented view of life in every sphere – our cultural identities, our daily lives, even our very psyches. We cling to our separate identities – whether national, ethnic, religious, racial, or political – and defend our self-interest to the detriment of the interests of humanity. We insist on lifestyles that poison the environment, threaten the well-being and even survival of future generations, waste precious resources for short-term gain, and cling to purely materialistic means to measure success. We define happiness in economic terms and the pursuit of consumer goods as a natural and reasonable way to find fulfillment in life, with absolute disregard for the needs of our spirit. Now, however, the society built on this worldview is disintegrating before our very eyes. We have come to a point in our collective development where unlimited national sovereignty and self-interest are dangerously impinging on the welfare of the planet and all human beings. It is only logical that we need to embrace a more inclusive vision of the human family and our place in it.

The new paradigm, supported by ample scientific evidence, is growing and is gradually gaining greater ascendancy. The paradigm is organic, acknowledging the oneness, wholeness and interconnectedness of all that exists. It is based on cooperation, mutualism, and collaboration. It embraces the truth that our individual welfare is intimately and inextricably connected to the welfare of humanity. It recognizes that humanity is organic with the world, and that the life of humans cannot be separated from the environment but, rather, is based on mutual interactions. It affirms that humanity's material well-being cannot be separated from other spheres of life; rather, it is intimately connected to its intellectual, social, ethical and spiritual well-being. In fact, the material well-being of humanity is impossible without regard for moral and ethical considerations. This holistic paradigm demands a new approach to the way we organize our society – one in which the foundation rests on moral, not materialistic, principles.

> *Science points beyond such a view [fragmentation], toward a one-ness of the universe which includes not only our natural environment but also our fellow human beings. I believe that the worldview implied by modern physics is inconsistent with our present society, which does not reflect the harmonious interrelatedness we observe in nature. To achieve such a state of dynamic balance, a radically different social and economic structure will be needed: a cultural revolution in the true sense of the word. The survival of our whole civilization may depend on whether we can bring about such a change.[13]*
>
> *– Fritjof Capra*

Just as an individual develops in stages, moving from childhood to adolescence to adulthood, humanity has also passed through the collective stages of childhood and adolescence, and is now poised on the threshold of collective maturity. The rebelliousness and upheavals so prevalent in today's society are characteristics of humanity's adolescence that soon must give way to the stability and wisdom of maturity.

This gradual maturation of humanity through the millennia has been characterized by the development of ever more complex social organization, integrating ever more diverse and greater numbers of people. Thus, social organization has progressed from simple units such as the family and tribe, to more complex units such as city-states and nations. We are now moving at a rapid pace toward a truly planetary society.

As in the life of a human being, this stage of maturity brings with it new challenges and demands, as well as new possibilities. Countries and the groups within them must learn to widen their vision and fully recognize their interdependence and the concomitant truth that the well-being of each depends on the well-being of all. They must learn to coordinate efforts, transcend their limited interests, and act effectively to solve problems that no one country can resolve by itself — problems such as environmental degradation, financial instability, drug-trafficking, terrorism, poverty, etc.

While we have been resisting the inevitable changes required of us, at some point, change will become inevitable. Population growth, by itself, will accentuate problems of resource scarcity, extremes of wealth and poverty, and inter-cultural tensions. According to a 2013 United Nations report, the world's population is predicted to increase to almost ten billion by 2050, with the added numbers coming from the less developed parts of the world. Such a world, with populations no longer isolated one from the other, but interconnected with instantaneous communication, increasingly efficient travel, and ever increasing migration, cannot survive, let alone thrive, with the antiquated leadership models that are already at woeful odds with the needs of our age. Without significant change, human societies will be subject to the tyranny of leaders who are narrowly focused on their own individual, cultural and national interests.

The crises we face are of such proportions that a transformative shift in our individual and collective consciousness is inevitable. Clearly, we need a more sustainable path to the future. As individuals and as societies we have a choice -- either become the agents and leaders of this change or face the impending chaos that will engulf us all.

THE PROCESSES OF INTEGRATION AND DISINTEGRATION

This time of transition is fraught with upheavals. To some extent these are natural and unavoidable, considering the magnitude of the changes involved. But the intensity of the upheavals and the suffering they cause also depend to a significant degree on us. We can facilitate this period of transition if we accept the needed changes and work for their implementation, or we can magnify the pain if we stubbornly cling to outmoded patterns of thought and action no longer viable in a world that has shrunk into a neighborhood.

The dialectic of acceptance of and resistance to these evolutionary changes gives birth to two parallel processes that are dramatically shaping humanity's fate and altering the course of its history. One is essentially an integrative process, while the other is fundamentally disruptive. The process of integration originates in actions and philosophies that seek to promote cooperation and unity at all levels of society, as an expression of the growing consciousness that the human race is one organic whole — an awareness that is in tune with the spirit of our age. The process of disintegration, on the other hand, results from the failure of antiquated social structures and systems of thought to respond to the accelerating pace of change and the urgent global crises that have characterized the 20th and now the 21st centuries.

The joint operation of these twin processes, that apparently oppose one another, release forces that are driving humanity toward the same end: the establishment of a global community. As the forces liberated by both processes accelerate and broaden the range of their impact, they produce profound changes in the ordered life of humankind and simultaneously give rise to both fear and hope for the future.

We are all too familiar with the problems that either provoke or are consequences of the process of disintegration – prejudice, oppression of minorities, extremes of wealth and poverty, destruction of the environment, delinquency and crime, corruption and immorality, feelings of hopelessness and meaninglessness – to name but a few critical examples. In their very severity, however, the problems generated by the process of disintegration have certain positive effects. They tear down walls that have historically divided peoples. They heighten our consciousness that the whole human family must consult and cooperate in attempts to find and apply solutions to global problems that concern and affect all. Consequently, the very suffering of humanity seems to bring about an awareness of the new lessons that must be learned. Thus, the process of disintegration serves to plow the soil of hearts and minds, preparing them to receive the seeds of the new paradigm.

While the disintegrative process has been clearing the ground, new evidences of the integrative process are simultaneously emerging. Notable examples are the development of the United Nations and its manifold agencies as well as the numerous transnational global bodies working to address the various crises confronting humanity, whether in health, the environment, energy, finance, poverty, or development. Some of these initiatives have already demonstrated quite dramatically that it is possible to address global crises through global collaborative efforts. Excellent examples of this can be seen in the successful fight against infectious diseases, particularly in the eradication of the scourge of smallpox from the planet and the near victory against polio, measles, guinea worm disease, and river blindness.

Another example of efforts in the right direction can be seen in the conference convened at the United Nations General Assembly in June 2009 regarding the world financial crisis. The purpose was to protect humanity from future financial roller-coaster types of catastrophes that have, in recent years, wiped out the wealth of many nations. The General Assembly President in his remarks warned against complacency and affirmed that he believed, "the Assembly was on the verge of taking a new step towards a human family that was focused on economic and ecological justice and 'which is united within itself, nature and Mother Earth'."[14] While we are still far from addressing most global crises effectively, as the conditions continue to deteriorate, there seems to be a commensurate increase in awareness of the oneness of humanity and the need for social justice. This is reflected in the rising frequency of urgent appeals for cooperation and unity coming from transnational organizations and global forums convened to address the multiple challenges threatening humanity's future well-being. The change in language reflects a growing consciousness of the oneness of humanity.

A quick review of statements and publications regarding various global efforts will reveal that they are all, in one way or another, calling for transformation, collaboration and a new kind of leadership. In his address to the Executive Assembly of the World Energy Council in 2009, the Council's president, Pierre Gadonneix, noted: "Across the globe, people will need to change their behaviour, not an easy thing to accomplish. There's a big difference between agreeing with a principle and making it part of our daily lives. In order for new policies to be successfully implemented, we must learn to listen, and in turn educate and explain, developing a sense of collective responsibility and fostering understanding...."[15] These and similar initiatives in all spheres of human endeavor may well represent the essential prelude to more comprehensive and bolder plans to ensure just and effective policies on a global scale.

Simultaneously, the proliferation of grassroots social movements working to promote peace, human rights, gender equity, sustainable development, universal education and other needed social and economic initiatives are gaining in strength and influence in all parts of the world. These have given birth to an ever-increasing number of non-governmental development organizations that work to promote these positive integrative processes at the local, regional, national, and international levels. These movements and organizations are significant indicators of the growing capacity of common people to come together, create, and direct innovative social structures that contribute to individual and social transformation.

Faced with these twin processes of integration and disintegration, each of us has three possible responses:

1) We can be *part of the problem*, allowing ourselves to be swept along by the wave of corruption, escapism, and excessive nationalism. We may justify our actions, asserting that, "everyone else does it" and what we are doing has "very minor" impact.

2) We can be *spectators,* watching the news and lamenting the state of the world, but taking no action to change anything because we feel there is "nothing we can do."

3) We can be *agents of transformation* who are part of the solution, consciously contributing to the process of integration.

In truth, most of us probably participate to some degree in each of these positions. If, to date, we have not done more to be agents of transformation, it may be because we are not sure of what to do or where to begin. However, the gravity of the crisis of our times demands that a growing number of people make a conscious effort to contribute to the process of integration. Transformative leadership offers one way of doing so.

If we wish to be agents of transformation, we must become aware that our efforts, no matter how small they may seem, do have an effect. In his study of the rise and fall of civilizations, Arnold Toynbee[16] emphasized the significant role of a *creative minority* during a period of transition, in which a once-dominant civilization sinks into a process of accelerating disintegration. At those times, a creative minority with a clear vision of the principles upon which a new civilization must be built, can have an effect far out of proportion to its numbers. Indeed, studies of *critical mass* indicate that once a sufficient number of people adopt an innovation in a social system, the rate of adoption becomes self-sustaining and creates further growth.[17] With time there comes a *tipping point* at which there is a sudden shift and the vast majority of the population accepts and begins to practice a beneficial innovation.[18]

Biologist Rupert Sheldrake explains how this may happen. He proposes that there is a kind of 'collective memory' that is not stored in the brain. When similar thoughts and actions are repeated, they give rise to characteristic structures and activities — "morphic fields" — that become accessible to others through "morphic resonance," allowing past knowledge to become present.[19] When enough individuals adopt a certain behavior, the memory of that behavior becomes more accessible to subsequent individuals and they are more likely to adopt it.

In light of these recent scientific insights, rather than becoming discouraged by the fewness of our numbers, we need to do all we can to contribute to the process of integration, with complete assurance that our efforts are not only worthwhile but will also have an ever-increasing impact in the construction of the emerging planetary society and will contribute to humanity's collective evolution.

THE NEED FOR MORAL LEADERSHIP

THE MOST BEAUTIFUL HOME IN THE WORLD

There was once a man who was busy building a home for himself. He wanted it to be the nicest, warmest, coziest home in the world.

Someone came to him to ask for help because the world was on fire. But it was his home he was interested in, not the world.

When he finally built his home, he found he did not have a planet to put it on.[20]

Organizations exerting efforts to solve the complex problems afflicting humanity have discovered that scientific, technological, and political means alone are insufficient to effect change. At the heart of the global crisis afflicting humanity is an underlying crisis of values. This crisis generates a vacuum in moral leadership that pervades all levels of society.

In 1987, the World Health Organization evaluated the first decade of its global plan to provide *Health for All by the Year 2000*. The evaluation determined that the first decade of the plan was a failure in the sense that not a single country in the world had established a primary health care system for all of its inhabitants during that period.

> *The strategy to achieve health for all (implies) the genera-*
> *tion of moral leadership, which is generally lacking in many*
> *societies.* [21]
>
> — *World Health Organization*

The evaluation concluded that the failure was not for lack of sci-entific knowledge, since primary health services require very basic knowledge. Neither was it a lack of appropriate administrative models nor a lack of financial resources that was responsible. None of these was the cause of the failure of the first decade of the plan. Rather, the main problem was the lack of *moral leadership* at all levels in the ministries of health throughout the world — a moral leadership com-mitted to the values underlying the plan, such as social justice, equity, and participation. What was missing was leadership sufficiently com-mitted to these values to be able to inspire sustained efforts to effect the budgetary and structural changes needed to set up primary health care systems for the most needy, a *moral* leadership willing to face the personal risks inherent in dealing with resistance to change.

Therefore, it is apparent that we need a clear definition of what we mean by "moral leadership." We will begin by submitting some basic criteria, based on the ideas presented thus far, of some aspects of moral leadership:

1) A deep awareness of the processes of disintegration and in-tegration leading humanity toward a global society and con-scious alignment with the process of integration;

2) A clear vision of a just institution or society and of the capa-bilities needed to make that vision a reality;

3) A commitment to both personal and collective transformation, striving to develop relevant capabilities and to exemplify ethical principles in both social and professional relationships.

The type of moral leadership we wish to promote is not only aligned with moral values and ethical principles, but is committed to a transformation from habitual patterns to empowering and proactive practices aligned with both evidence and ethics. It implies a fundamental shift in worldview and a commitment to learning and service to the common good. We will call this kind of leadership *transformative leadership*.

CHAPTER II

MENTAL MODELS OF

HUMAN NATURE AND SOCIETY

Many of us believe that today's human problems will never be solved, that they have simply gotten too big for solutions of any kind or that, even if we solved them temporarily, human nature cannot itself change and therefore we would just get into the same mess again....

Hopeless pessimism often comes from lack of perspective. If we look at things narrowly — from within a difficult situation — they may well seem hopeless, but if we manage to step out of our dark hole, so to speak, to gain some perspective on ourselves within it, we may begin to see a way out.

What could be more interesting, more exciting, than to be alive in the very age when we as a species have the opportunity to mature, to solve the adolescent problems we have caused ourselves and others? [1]

– Elisabet Sahtouris

In the last chapter, we studied the need to analyze and question our mental models, in order to keep them from blinding us to the emerging paradigm that is a sign of our times. The most fundamental of these mental models are the ways in which we view ourselves and the societies in which we live. We carry all kinds of unexamined assumptions about who we are, what kind of world we live in, and what are the possibilities for us as individuals and for us collectively. There is a dynamic relationship between our mental model of human nature and our mental model of society. Those qualities that define us as human beings will necessarily also define us collectively, with reciprocal influences on one another. Therefore, we need to begin by questioning the mental models we have about who we are as human beings and how that relates to the societies we have created.

Many view human beings as aggressive and selfish by nature. Mental models of society that accept egotism and competition as the norm and ignore evidence showing that the advancement of civilization throughout history has been based on cooperation reinforce this view of human nature. These mental models of human nature and society have given rise to attitudes and behaviors that are no longer useful in today's interdependent world community. Therefore, before exploring further, we will reflect upon the power of mental models to understand the importance of questioning them deeply and transforming them when their flaws are revealed.

The work of Douglas McGregor in management highlights the power of mental models and how they tend to create the very realities they predict. McGregor states that managers' assumptions (mental models) about human nature influence their approach to human resource management in the workplace. He maintains that all managers have such assumptions, even if they are not aware of them.

He identifies two groups of assumptions, which he calls Theory X and Theory Y.

Theory X, the conventional managerial approach, states that "workers need to be motivated and controlled through direct pressure from management because they are lazy, lack ambition, dislike responsibility, prefer to be told what to do, and passively resist achieving the goals of the organization. Money is the only way to motivate them."[2]

Theory Y advocates another set of managerial assumptions regarding workers. It proposes, "when given a chance, people are self-motivated to meet the organization's goals while working towards personal growth and development. Their characteristics are the opposite of those assumed by Theory X. Theory Y further maintains that if people appear to behave according to the characteristics posed by Theory X, it is only because the organization in which they work requires them to do so. According to this viewpoint, a manager's task is to arrange matters in such a way that people can fulfill their needs for self-realization and achievement in the process of meeting the goals of the organization."[3]

The point we want to highlight is that our assumptions about human nature greatly affect the way we see and treat others. Furthermore, these suppositions tend to be self-fulfilling prophecies. In the case of the workers, they respond to their managers' assumptions by exhibiting the characteristics expected of them. That is why there is no point in referring to actual behavior to prove the validity of a mental model about human nature, whether it is positive or negative, because each model engenders the very outcomes that would seem to validate it. Instead, we can: 1) reflect on the consequences of each model and its positive or negative impacts on society and 2) examine scientific evidence to determine to what extent the model coincides with data. Then we can consciously replace our flawed mental models with an evidence-based conceptual framework.

In the following sections, we will engage in critical analysis of some of the prevailing mental models about human nature that have influenced our ways of thinking and acting and have resulted in the societies in which we live.

MENTAL MODELS OF HUMAN NATURE

▶ Man as a Rational Animal

In most Western societies, the mental model of man as a rational animal prevails. Some advocates of this model emphasize what we share with animals. Others highlight rationality as the distinctive human trait that makes us qualitatively different from animals. In both cases, man is studied from a purely material perspective, without contemplating the existence of a soul or human spirit, or considering human existence to have any essential purpose beyond survival and reproduction.

We will study a few variants of this approach, critically analyze some of the theories that have resulted, and explore some of the faulty thinking involved.

▶▶ Survival of the Fittest

In his mid-19th century study on *The Origin of Species,* Charles Darwin proposed that organisms having certain features were more likely to survive and reproduce than others, and that eventually this resulted in the "natural selection" of those hereditary traits and their generalization in that species. Shortly thereafter, Herbert Spencer suggested that this process resulted in the "survival of the fittest" in the struggle for life,[4] which Spencer extended into the realms of sociology and ethics.

Despite Darwin's objections, these concepts were applied to human society under the name of "Social Darwinism," which proposed that the processes of natural selection and survival of the fittest would have favored the most aggressive, violent, ambitious, and greedy individuals, resulting in the predominance of these features among human beings. This evokes images of brutish cavemen clobbering each other with clubs until the winner becomes chief of the tribe and carries the women away to produce more belligerent cavemen to continue the fight. As a result, these characteristics have supposedly become deeply ingrained in 'human nature.'

In reality, it is our capacity for cooperation that has enabled human life to continue, as only through mutual assistance has it been possible to overcome hunger and the rigors of nature. Actually, the term "survival of the fittest" does not refer to the strongest and most aggressive, as many believe, but to the ability to adapt to the demands of the environment. Consequently, it is not logical to assert that conflict, aggression and selfishness played a role in the survival of the human species, nor that they prevailed in our evolution. Just as the ability to cooperate and be of mutual assistance has been necessary in order to reach this point in history, the future of humanity will also depend on the prevalence of these characteristics, both individually and collectively.

> *It is scientifically incorrect to say that in the course of hu-*
> *man evolution there has been a selection for aggressive behav-*
> *ior more than for other kinds of behavior. In all well-studied*
> *species, status within the group is achieved by the ability to*
> *cooperate and to fulfill social functions relevant to the structure*
> *of that group. When…hyper-aggressive animals are present in*
> *a social group, they either disrupt its social structure or are*
> *driven out. Violence is neither in our evolutionary legacy nor*
> *in our genes.*[5]
>
> — *Seville Statement on Violence*

In 1986, twenty scientists from a variety of disciplines including biology, sociology, psychology, psychiatry, neurophysiology, and genetics, came together from around the world and produced the *Seville Statement on Violence,* concluding that there is no scientific evidence to support that organized human violence is biologically determined. In 1989, UNESCO officially adopted this document. The document concludes, "Just as wars begin in the minds of men, peace also begins in our minds. The same species who invented war is capable of inventing peace. The responsibility lies with each of us."[6]

▶▶ GENETIC DETERMINISM

The science of genetics arose in the late 19th and early 20th centuries through the studies of Gregor Mendel and William Bateson, followed by the discovery of chromosomes and the structure of DNA by Watson and Crick in 1953. These developments fit in well with the theory of natural selection, as they provided the mechanism through which physiological traits were inherited.

As was to be expected, it was not long before speculations arose regarding an alleged genetic programming of certain aspects of human behavior, particularly selfishness, aggression, and territorialism. During the 1970s, there was even an attempt to raise these ideas to the status of science under the name of "Sociobiology." Since it was assumed that all traits were transmitted through genetic material, scientists anticipated that there must be well over 100,000 genes to encode the diversity of traits. However, the Human Genome Project, completed in 2003, identified only 20,000 to 25,000 genes, far short of the number expected. Clearly, genes were not an adequate explanation for all human traits. The development of *epigenetics* — "the study of heritable changes in gene function that occur without a change in the DNA sequence"[7] — suggested that some traits and behaviors resulting even from a parent's *experiences* can also be passed to future generations, in the form of *epigenetic phenomena.*[8] Both the relatively limited number of genes as well as the discovery of epigenetics, which allows for extra-chromosomal transmission of traits, undermine the argument for genetic determinism.

▶▶ DETERMINISM AND FATALISM

This brings us to two other closely related mental models: *determinism* and *fatalism.* The erroneous understanding of the implications of the "survival of the fittest" and genetic influences on behavior has led some to conclude that we are *pre-determined* to act in certain ways due to circumstances beyond our control. A belief in genetic programming, inherent aggression, or innate selfishness would consider these to be internal determinants of our behavior. Others emphasize external determinants, such as the impersonal forces of our sociocultural surroundings. Still others believe that everything that happens to us in life is predetermined by *fate*, negating man's free will. Fatalism and determinism share the same harmful effects, as they present destiny as something unavoidable to which we must submit. This turns us into passive subjects and helpless victims of forces beyond our control.

Those who hold deterministic or fatalistic mental models tend to blame destiny or the environment for harmful behaviors, instead of seeing individuals as responsible for their actions. As a result, these models lead to an abdication of accountability. When people see themselves as victims of their circumstances, lacking control over their own lives and actions, they tend to blame others for their problems, be it the government, the economy, an unfavorable environment, or a lack of parental love. They have little reason to exercise their willpower and take responsibility for their own actions and the resulting consequences. This is not to deny the influence of our heredity or the environment on our development. What is erroneous about determinism is its tendency to de-emphasize the need and potential for personal transformation and to leave the responsibility for social change in the hands of others outside the immediate environment. Likewise, rather than the fatalistic stance of "resigning ourselves to fate," we can choose the healthier view that everything that happens to us in life – whether we like it or not – can ultimately contribute to our growth and maturation. With such an outlook, we can choose to learn from our negative life experiences instead of merely bearing them as heavy loads.

▶▶ IMPLICATIONS OF THE RATIONAL ANIMAL MENTAL MODEL

The mental model of man as a rational animal views humans as essentially self-centered, greedy, and competitive beings who will resort to aggression and even violence should their self-interest be threatened. Unfortunately this purely material view of the human being has rapidly spread throughout the world and has affected the development of all nations, leaving few societies untouched. It has so permeated the development agenda of multilateral agencies and donor organizations that it has eroded the cultural viability of traditional societies. This materialistic worldview has not only failed in raising people out of poverty, in creating prosperity, or advancing human happiness, but there is ample evidence that it has, in fact, been responsible for *decreasing* collective prosperity and resulting in greater personal dissatisfaction with life.[9]

Furthermore, these assumptions about the nature of man in society fail to take into account the numerous studies affirming our prosocial tendencies. Research in psychology has shown that human beings have natural empathic tendencies from infancy. For example, at one year, children show concern when someone else is hurt or sad. By the age of two, they can distinguish their own feelings from those of others, but still seek to console others who show signs of pain, and their empathic emotions are more complex.[10] Empathy may be regarded as part of a more inclusive pro-social personality trait that develops in children and motivates helping behaviors into young adulthood.[11]

Some theorists suggest that viewing another's emotional state automatically activates our personal associations with that state, causing us to react to another's experience as we would to our own.[12] These studies conclude that the tendency to be concerned about others is just as natural in human beings as worrying about ourselves. This does not mean that people are not capable of having self-centered, avaricious, or even antisocial attitudes. Human beings can exhibit a broad range of behaviors, from the most selfish to the most altruistic, which demonstrates the cultural and learned nature of any predominance of these traits. In fact, there are many factors that contribute to the development of such characteristics in a person. The most powerful of these influences come from the examples and comments of parents and other significant role models. Due to its pervasiveness, mass media also has a powerful influence.

In brief, there is no scientific proof to support the notion that human beings are selfish by nature. Although we can certainly behave that way, we are also fully capable of sincere, selfless concern for the well-being of others. Whether we practice the one or the other depends partly on the way we were raised and partly on our own decisions.

▶ Metaphysical Nature of Man

We have seen that the mental model of man as a rational animal that is selfish by nature not only lacks a scientific basis, but also acts as a self-fulfilling prophecy that reinforces a culture of greed and violence. Metaphysical theories about human nature also exist. These can be grouped into three categories: innate evil, inherent goodness and a dual nature.

▶▶ Innate Evil

According to a concept that is deeply entrenched, especially in Western societies, human beings are inherently 'bad.' Different explanations are sometimes given to support this point of view. Some see man as a fallen angel who must strive to return to his original condition in heaven. Others believe that man has inherited a sin that was committed by the common forebears of all humankind. Still others believe a 'devil' has been allowed to reign in the human world for a certain length of time. Finally there are those who, observing the situation of the world, conclude that a flaw in the human soul compels human beings to wickedness.

These notions, despite their diverse variations and origins, share the recognition that as human beings we commit acts that go against our individual and collective well-being. This recognition can lead to humility, allowing the admission of our own weaknesses, imperfections and need for support. It can also lead to a healthy attitude of tolerance, understanding and compassion regarding the faults of others.

However, believing our human spirit to be 'bad' by nature can also lead to a feeling of shame and hopelessness — that no matter how hard we may try, there is no escape from this inherent evil. Furthermore, a belief in man's inherent wickedness can be used as an excuse to avoid responsibility to improve, under the pretext that we are 'only human,' or blaming 'the devil' that 'got into me.' In the collective, this focus tends to emphasize the need for controlling or eradicating faults or problems, rather than cultivating potential goodness and better ways of interacting.

▶▶ INHERENT GOODNESS

A second concept, more common among Eastern cultures, is that human beings are essentially 'good.' This category also includes a broad range of ideas. Some simply say that by definition since God is good, His creation must also necessarily be good. Therefore, humanity cannot be bad. Others believe that the human soul can evolve spiritually until it becomes God, or that humans are already a part of God (understood as the sum total of all existing things). To explain the existence of evil in the world, some respond that although humans are created good, society has a corrupting influence.

These notions also share certain positive implications. They can lead to accepting that we all have the potential to behave morally in ways that benefit all. They also have the effect of promoting a positive self-image. They focus our attention on the seeds of goodness growing in each person with the resultant development of positive qualities. Finally, they tend to enhance initiatives to improve the human condition, as they center efforts more on cultivating virtues than on attacking defects.

However, the concept of man's inherent goodness can also lead to error. For example, some educators who followed this philosophy believed that children's inherent goodness should be left to blossom naturally without adult intervention. But, in reality, children need help to channel and discipline their natural traits and capabilities, and to avoid negative attitudes and behaviors. Furthermore, on a larger scale, these assumptions may dissuade some from combating the evils in society if they think that man's inherent goodness means that these problems will solve themselves over time.

▶▶ A Dual Nature

A third concept of human nature is that man has a dual nature. On the one hand, latent in the human soul lies the potential for all of the virtues, such as love, wisdom, justice, mercy, compassion, etc. This aspect of human beings, which could be called the higher nature or noble essence, would explain the statement that we "are created in God's image" — that is, within the human heart lie the seeds of saintly qualities that reflect the attributes of God.

On the other hand, as human beings we also have an insistent self that goads us to selfish attitudes and harmful behaviors. This aspect of our being, which could be called our lower nature, is what drags us down towards hatred, divisiveness, oppression, injustice, perversity and corruption. The soul, like a mirror, can reflect the vices of the lower nature, or turn towards the higher nature and reflect increasingly noble qualities.

These two human facets, continually struggling with each other, have provided themes for great poetry and literature throughout the ages. It is as though our higher nature or essential nobility provides the motivation and energy to lift us up while our lower nature works in the opposite direction, dragging us down and slowing our progress.

The concepts of innate evil or inherent goodness do not necessarily motivate us to actively cultivate virtues, because in response to the former, we may emphasize attacking what is 'bad' while under the influence of the latter, we may wait for goodness to blossom naturally. In contrast, the understanding of a dual nature in human beings demands that we nurture those positive qualities that ennoble us, while controlling those that debase us. Just as we light a lamp to illumine the night, we can overcome our vices by developing virtues to replace them.

If we potentially possess all the virtues, then our true destiny consists of developing those qualities that lie latent within our beings, just as the fate of a seed is to become a great tree, full of leaves, flowers and fruits. We know that a seed needs to be carefully planted and patiently cultivated in order to reveal its full potential and so fulfill its inherent destiny. Similarly, effort is needed to bring to light all of the marvelous qualities that lie hidden within human beings.

That part of our nature that we nurture is the one that will grow. Will it be our higher nature or our lower nature? The choice is ours.

THE TWO DOGS

A boy asked his wise old grandfather: "Why is it that we sometimes do good and at times are bad?"

His grandfather responded, "Within each of us, there are two dogs — a good one and a bad one — who are continually struggling with one another. When the good dog is on top we do noble deeds; but when the bad one is winning, we commit shameful acts."

The boy pondered a while, then asked: "Which dog is going to win?"

The grandfather answered: "That depends on us and which dog we feed."

MENTAL MODELS OF SOCIETY

▶ COMPETITION

Just as there are mental models of human nature, there are also mental models of human culture and society. In the West, the prevailing cultural theme is one of competition and contest. This predominant theme, in fact, is at the foundation of the free market concept of capitalism. Michael Karlberg, a leading voice in the critique of competitive cultures, explores the fundamentally adversarial underpinnings of Western liberal democracies in his book, *Beyond the Culture of Contest*. He explains that these dynamics proliferate throughout all spheres of life – economics, politics, the legal system, the educational system, mass media, athletic events, even the arts and social interactions – and come to characterize a ubiquitous "culture of contest."[13]

Guided by this model, individuals and institutions pursue their interests through contests in which the one with the most power, resources or influence 'wins.' These systems based on competition tend to generate inequalities and injustices, as they generally benefit those who are already winning, while those in need of more support are left further and further behind. For example, in today's economic system, the more money we have, the easier it is to earn more, while the fewer resources we have, the harder it is to escape from poverty. The result is the present situation, in which 10% of the world's population owns 85% of the world's household wealth, while the richest 1% alone account for 40% of the world's assets. In contrast, the poorest 50% of the world's population owns barely 1% of global wealth.[14] These extremes of wealth and poverty are not only fundamentally unjust but also contribute to crime, terrorism and economic instability.

Despite the serious problems caused by competition, many believe that it is inevitable – an essential feature of human life. One common argument in defense of competition as an organizing principle of society is that it supposedly increases performance. The fact is, however, that it only motivates the upper 5% while discouraging the other 95% who have little chance of winning. Numerous studies have shown that the most productive way to work is cooperating in teams, followed by independent work, while the least productive is competing against others.[15] The stress involved in seeking to beat someone else wastes energy and distracts from efforts to improve, whereas working in cooperative teams creates synergy. Groups based on collaboration and reciprocity also achieve much more rapid progress than the combined efforts of the same number of individuals working alone. The whole is, indeed, greater than the sum of its parts.

People often mistakenly associate competition with excellence. However, studies have shown that quality is best promoted using *intrinsic* motivators (desire to serve, love of excellence), and is harmed by *extrinsic* motivators (money, awards, prestige).[16] Competition, being an extrinsic motivator (the reward is winning), not only has a limited effect, it also damages intrinsic motivation. In contrast, cooperation produces several intrinsic motivators, including the enjoyment of shared success, the satisfaction of cultivating positive relationships with others, and the feeling of responsibility towards other members of an interdependent team. True excellence is promoted through cooperation and impaired by competition.

Given the bankruptcy of competition as a social norm, numerous alternative proposals have been put forward based on win-win relationships in which each person's achievements do not undermine possibilities for others, but rather increase their chances of success. These systems include innovative economic and political approaches, horizontal forms of leadership, teamwork, cooperative learning, cooperative games, religious ecumenism, and many more. The *Transformative Leadership* program elaborated in this book seeks to give both interpersonal relations and social structures a more cooperative focus.

▶ ADVERSARIAL SOCIETY

Michael Karlberg explains that in a *culture of contest*, the outcomes are rarely just. To address the injustice that inevitably arises, the culture of contest is surrounded by a *culture of protest*. The protested injustice then becomes the pivot of another contest, which, in turn, will result in additional protest. In this mental model the world is viewed through the lens of *scarcity*, which assumes there is not enough for everyone. The internal dialogue goes something like this: "I better get as much as I can as quickly as possible. If I don't get my share, others will take it and I will be left with nothing. I will protect my rights and even fight for what is rightfully mine. There will always be winners and losers and I will do whatever is necessary, even if I have to step on others, to win. I don't want to be a loser."

There is, however, an alternative way to view the world that is never considered in an adversarial mind-set — that is through the lens of *abundance* – that there is plenty for everyone, if we choose to see it and live that way.

The adversarial worldview further reinforces the mental model of man either as a rational animal or as a victim of social forces beyond his control. These mental models of human nature generate social structures that in turn confirm and reinforce the very behaviors they predict, leading to a dynamic interplay between the individual and society that cannot be dissected into cause and effect. Today the adversarial model based on the pursuit of self-interest is so deeply ingrained into the culture that it seems natural, inevitable, and inescapable. In fact, for those whose daily experience is so deeply immersed in this environment, another model of human and social interaction may seem unrealistic and utopian, even unnatural.

However, there are ample examples in human history of widely accepted cultural practices that gradually became obsolete and were eradicated. Good examples of these are the abolition of slavery and the achievement of universal suffrage. Although the denial of human rights to segments of the population at one time seemed natural and inevitable, now virtually all countries of the world agree on a set of basic rights for all people, even though they may not adhere to it themselves. Furthermore, as the old paradigm begins to shift, new models, structures and institutions supporting the new understandings arise and take root. If we look for these signs in contemporary society, we will see examples of initiatives based on mutual benefit and reciprocity increasing in scope and number. Examples of these can be found in global movements to protect the environment, reverse global warming, develop more sustainable lifestyles, advocate for human rights, promote health, overcome poverty, and fight corruption, to name a few.

▶ RACISM

Racism is a pernicious example of the adversarial mental model that divides the world into 'us' and 'them.' There are, of course, other examples of prejudice that are also destructive, but racism is particularly divisive. It is a blight that has plagued humanity throughout history and still contaminates human relationships. The racist view of humankind maintains that people's character, capacity and value are racially determined. It claims that racial differences are due to differential evolution, which has provided some races with greater intellectual and physical endowments than others, resulting in inherent superiority, due to unalterable circumstances of birth.

Often those who believe they are superior assume that members of the 'inferior' race are there to serve them and relieve them of toilsome tasks. This makes it hard for them to develop an attitude of respect and service towards members of that race. Since they think that the 'inferiority' is genetically determined, it is also hard for them to believe in the inherent potential of the members of that 'race.' When they do help them to develop their capacities, it is often with a certain degree of condescension. When those of the 'inferior race' develop capabilities on their own, racists may feel that they have forgotten 'their place' or 'who they are,' and react with fear, resentment or hatred. It is easy for racists to justify giving special privileges to those whom they consider superior, while denying them to those they perceive as being inferior and undeserving. They may even deprive them of their fundamental human rights. In this way, racism erodes the basic values of justice and unity.

When people interiorize self-concepts of inferiority, they may doubt their own capabilities and find it difficult to develop them. Since they often associate service with servitude and humiliation, they may have a hard time acquiring a spirit of service motivated by love. They will often harbor feelings of mistrust, resentment and/or hatred towards the dominant group. No matter how justifiable these negative feelings may be, they interfere with the development of healthier attitudes and hamper progress towards a society based on justice.

Even more damaging than its impacts on individuals are the consequences of racism on society as a whole. It has been the primary cause of slavery, countless wars, and pogroms of systematic genocide. Even when it has not reached those extremes, it has often been a cause of systematic structural discrimination. In some countries, the racist model has been perpetuated in a more dissimulated fashion through the structuring of social classes. Although a society may not admit to having racist attitudes, racial proportions in each social class reveal that wealth distribution correlates strongly with color or caste. People having a racist mental model – albeit unconsciously – will tend to expect preferential treatment for the favored race and discriminate against the one that is deemed inferior.

Racism directly contradicts the *oneness of the human race*, a fundamental principle of the age in which we live, and a truth confirmed by all sciences. The basic sciences as well as the social sciences all recognize a single human species, although infinitely diverse in the secondary aspects of life.

▶ NATURALIZING THE SOCIAL ORDER

ISN'T IT NATURAL TO HAVE THESE SPOTS?

Once upon a time, there was a village where all of the inhabitants had a disease that caused spots on their skin. Since they all had the same illness, they thought that it was a natural characteristic of all human beings.

One day a physician came to the village. He did not have any spots, so the villagers viewed him as abnormal. He told them that they had a disease for which there was treatment. The villagers did not believe him until he cured one of them and the spots went away. When they realized that they were sick, they accepted the treatment and were cured.

Mental models are not confined to our minds, but are reflected in the way we act, our normative practices, and our political, economic and social structures. If we believe that human nature is incorrigibly aggressive and selfish, it will seem natural to structure our social relations in the form of power struggles to promote vested interests, as observed in many Western societies. As a result, there is much more violence in New York City, where people believe that anger cannot be controlled, than in Tokyo, where the prevailing worldview prescribes not only the possibility but also the imperative to avoid aggression. In this way, our beliefs about the nature of man and society become self-fulfilling prophecies. The assumption that aggression and selfishness are inevitable, encourages people to behave in violent, greedy ways. Similarly, the prevalence of social structures that institutionalize selfishness, greed, competition, and aggression have naturalized them to such a degree that alternative proposals based on other concepts of human nature are rejected outright without further analysis.

This naturalization of our sociocultural environment is a normal part of our upbringing. From birth, infants perceive not only the prevailing mental models in their sociocultural surroundings, but also countless tangible examples of how those mental models are put into practice. As they grow, children learn theories that support those mental models, see them modeled in common practices and honored institutions, and are continually exposed to their representations through the arts and mass media. These messages repeatedly reinforce a particular way of perceiving the world and acting within it, until people come to believe that it is not just one way, but the *only* way to think and act. They become convinced that it *is* the world, not just one representation of it.

We interiorize these social configurations to the point that they seem natural to us, a matter of common sense, inevitable and, therefore, impossible to change. Nevertheless, a culture in which greed and conflict prevail suffers from a kind of spiritual disease, which can be treated through the reeducation of its members and the restructuring of its institutions. The first step in transforming an adversarial culture is the denaturalization of structures that institutionalize greed and conflict. In the past, the denaturalization of institutions such as slavery and male chauvinism led to the understanding that they were not natural, inevitable features of society, but cultural constructs. This made it possible to promote a culture in which persons of color and the feminine sex were granted the same rights and prerogatives as white males.

In order to denaturalize dysfunctional cultural practices, first we must examine them carefully in order to dissociate ourselves from them. We need to realize that we have learned certain practices, but that there is a range of alternative ways to act in a given situation, many of which are practiced by other cultures. Only when we attain a level of objectivity that enables us to see certain social constructs as contingent and changeable, can we say that they have been denaturalized in our minds. Then we will be open to studying and testing alternative practices. We will know that our society is a product of our collective actions, which in turn are a direct consequence of our assumptions and beliefs. We will realize that the world has not always been the way it is today, that in the past one hundred years it has changed more than throughout the rest of human history, and that it can and will continue to change. We will understand that even within the most divided and egocentric cultures, there are numerous examples of human beings displaying reciprocity and cooperation.

INTERDEPENDENT PROCESSES

We have seen that our mental models about human nature tend to be consistent with those we have of culture and society. We also know that our mental models determine our behavior, and that the effects of our actions are what shape our world. Therefore, moving towards a more principle-centered world requires that we integrate two different processes. On the one hand, we need to change our mental models of human nature and modify our individual behaviors accordingly. On the other, we need to change our mental models regarding society, in order to promote new forms of social, political and economic organization.

We will refer to these two processes as *personal transformation* and *social transformation*. Neither is sufficient without the other. Rather, all efforts towards change need to work on these two fronts simultaneously. The top-down approach, that seeks personal transformation by changing social structures, rarely works in the long run because it tends to be perceived as an imposition and is met with resistance. Alternatively, the bottom-up approach, that pursues organizational reform through merely personal transformation, typically results in frustration, as it generates the will to change but does not establish the institutional arrangements needed to channel that volition towards the desired result.

For example, in the fight against corruption, activities often aim to impose a new organizational culture from above by establishing new regulations, laws and policies regarding transparency, prosecution, and penalization. Then these codes of conduct are socialized in an attempt to spread the new culture. The results are usually far from optimal. Although the measures are very necessary, they are not sufficient. A change only at the top often results in a 'work-around' at the bottom that subverts the expected benefit of the new regulations. Instead, there must be a change in the way people think and act, in order to support a culture of trust and transparency.

An example of an exclusively bottom-up approach would be seeking peace by changing the way individuals think and act without altering the social structures that perpetuate conflict within and among countries. This doesn't work either. Although the masses of humanity are basically gentle, peace-loving people, this changes neither the structures that promote political and economic conflict nor the institutional paradigms upon which such struggles are grounded.

However, if we exchange divisive mental models for a conceptual framework based on the potential for human nobility, we will recognize the unique contributions that each person can make to the well-being of all. We will see a holistic relationship between the person and society and a reciprocal interaction between the welfare of each individual and his impact on the good of the whole. We will recognize that enduring change will demand that we work on both fronts simultaneously.

CHAPTER III

DOMINANT MODELS OF LEADERSHIP

The number of books and articles that have proliferated related to leadership in recent decades, together with the programs and institutes devoted to training competent leaders, bear testimony to the desire for better leadership. Whenever there is a crisis with global fallout, a new call for effective leadership reverberates. And yet, new approaches frequently fall victim to old ways of thinking and acting. In order to gain a deeper understanding of what is missing, we will critically scrutinize prevailing mental models of leadership to better understand their limitations.

Leadership does not exist in a vacuum; it exists in the context of a group. Therefore, any discussion of leadership will be more relevant if we relate it to group dynamics, analyzing the effect that the leader has on group functioning. A group has three primary functions that help it to achieve its purpose. These are:

1) *to accomplish the tasks and objectives for which it was created;*

2) *to create and strengthen unity among its members;*

3) *to develop the capabilities of its members.*

Although everyone recognizes the importance of the first function, not all are conscious of the second and third functions. The importance of the second function, unity, becomes clear when we recall the functioning and achievements of a united group in which we participated and compare it to one where members were disunited. As to the third function, the more capabilities the members of the group have developed, the better they can contribute to institutional goals.

The effectiveness of the group depends on how well these functions are carried out. An organization that pays attention to all three will progress more than one that only concentrates on the first function. Therefore, every member who contributes to the realization of any of these functions can be said to exercise leadership, whether he has a formal position of authority in the group or not. When shared leadership is encouraged, the talents and capabilities of all members of the group are more fully utilized and the group functions with greater effectiveness and unity. Furthermore, shared leadership lessens competition and the struggle for power.

Not all styles of leadership, however, promote shared leadership, nor do they contribute equally to the accomplishment of the group's three main functions. Therefore, we can evaluate different models of leadership by the degree to which each contributes to the realization of these functions. We can classify the prevailing mental models of leadership into five major categories: *authoritarian, paternalistic, know-it-all, manipulative,* and *democratic.* In the following sections, we will briefly describe and analyze each model of leadership in terms of its characteristics, the typical reactions of group members, and how effectively it addresses the three group functions.

AUTHORITARIAN LEADERSHIP

REGULATIONS

A sergeant was asking a group of recruits why walnut was used for the butt of a rifle.

"Because it is harder than other wood," said one man.

"Wrong," said the sergeant.

"Because it is more elastic."

"Wrong again."

"Because it has a better shine."

"You boys certainly have a lot to learn. Walnut is used for the simple reason that it is laid down in the Regulations!" [1]

Authoritarian leaders give orders. They expect immediate, exact and unquestioned obedience to their authority. They avoid dialogue, do not allow questions, and offer no explanations. The prototype of the authoritarian leader is found in military organizations, although this mode of leadership is also commonly seen in traditional relationships between managers and employees.

Subordinates of an authoritarian leader usually feel resentment, which may be expressed either overtly or covertly. Resentment that is openly manifested may lead eventually to rebelliousness or revolt. Resentment that is suppressed may foster apparent submission and obedience, where the worker responds, "Yes, sir," similar to the "Yes, master" common in the days of slavery. Yet this apparent submission can hide a passive resistance that undermines the work at hand. Frequently, 'mysterious' obstructions arise for which no one accepts responsibility. In the leader's absence, tasks are often carried out slowly. Initiative is virtually unknown.

63

An authoritarian style of leadership does not foster group unity since it provokes resentment and rebelliousness. Because an authoritarian leader makes no effort to develop the capabilities of group members, the group as a whole fails to improve its effectiveness. Although an authoritarian leader may keep the group moving to complete routine, short-term goals, the lack of commitment on the part of group members will make it difficult to achieve long-term goals, or goals that demand quality work, creativity, or innovation.

At present, authoritarian leadership has fallen into disrepute, and few wish to be identified as authoritarian leaders. However, many continue to manifest characteristics of authoritarian leadership. These traits permeate leadership at all levels of society, even within the family unit, the 'workshop' where change must first begin. These lingering characteristics of authoritarian leadership may be among the most serious impediments to fostering the development of shared leadership. Furthermore, there is a difference between having a legitimate position of authority and acting in an authoritarian manner. Positions of authority exist, are necessary, and should be respected. However, those in a position of authority do not have to act in an authoritarian manner. In fact, they become more effective when they learn to exercise authority within the framework of shared leadership.

PATERNALISTIC LEADERSHIP

WHY DO SO MANY CHILDREN DIE?

While visiting a rural community, a friend was taken aback by the number of small crosses in the village cemetery, indicating a large number of childhood deaths. When he asked the villagers about it, they sadly confirmed that it was true, that many children died of sickness.

"What is the village doing to try to prevent so many deaths," asked the visitor.

"We are waiting for the government to come build a hospital," was the reply.

It had not occurred to anyone that they themselves could take any kind of initiative.[2]

Those who exercise a paternalistic mode of leadership may sincerely desire the well-being of group members and be motivated by genuine feelings of care and affection. However, they treat the members as overprotective parents would treat their children. They take care of them, protect them, remove all obstacles from their path, micromanage their tasks, and tell them not to worry, because they have already figured everything out. They might ask group members for their opinions and give the outward impression of being open-minded, but in the final analysis, they make the decisions.

Paternalistic leaders do not help group members develop their capabilities; indeed, they may not feel that the members have many capabilities. Rather, they derive satisfaction from knowing how greatly they are needed.

This model of leadership is commonly found in religious or charitable organizations, in government programs, and in some non-governmental development organizations. Leaders may even talk about promoting participation, but maintain control because they lack faith in the capabilities of the members and fear that things may get out of hand if members take initiative.

Paternalistic leadership cultivates attitudes of dependency and helplessness, paralyzing creative initiative and personal responsibility. The members turn to the leader to resolve all their problems without making any effort to be self-sufficient or to develop their own capabilities.

As long as paternalistic leaders actively meet the needs of other group members, unity and a competent execution of tasks may appear to exist. In reality, though, the group does not do the work. Everything depends on the great parent-leader. As a consequence, when a paternalistic leader leaves a group, it tends to disintegrate because nobody else in the group has developed the necessary capabilities, knowledge, experience, or initiative to carry on.

It may be very comfortable to be part of a group with a paternalistic leader. The leader does everything. The members of the group are taken care of and may also receive partial credit for the group's achievements. Group members become accustomed to the leader's care and may even come to expect it as their right. Therefore, the members of a group with paternalistic leadership are sometimes resistant to change that requires them to assume responsibility for themselves. If this mode of leadership suddenly ceases, they may complain, protest, or even demand another paternalistic leader. It often does not even occur to them that they could do something to help themselves. They tend to resist the idea even when it is presented. Why should they make an effort if they have the right to be taken care of?

When a new project is presented to a community that has come to depend on paternalistic interventions by well-meaning organizations, the first question that community members often ask is, "What benefits are you offering us?" If the new organization does not provide immediate, continuous material benefits, a community may not be interested in working for its own betterment.

Groups accustomed to paternalistic leadership cannot be transformed overnight into participatory organizations where decisions and responsibilities are shared. Often the members do not have the necessary capabilities or self-confidence. If change is to occur, all must adopt a new conceptual framework of leadership. The leader must provide encouragement, gradually help the members to develop capabilities, and give them progressively greater opportunities to take on more responsibility, until a truly shared mode of leadership develops.

KNOW-IT-ALL LEADERSHIP

Know-it-all leadership often occurs when there is a marked difference between the knowledge and experience of the leader and that of the other members of the group. As a result, the leader attempts to dominate the group based on his superior knowledge. This mode of leadership is often seen in academic circles, among teachers, consultants and technical advisors, and others who make their living by sharing their knowledge.

In their relationship with other group members, know-it-all leaders tend to seize every opportunity to boast of their knowledge, credentials, or previous experience. They like to display their wares. They often attempt to diminish the credibility of other members of the group by subtly ridiculing their ideas and suggestions, or by making jokes about them and their contributions. Simply by the way they act, know-it-all leaders try to let everybody know that they really are far more knowledgeable about the subject than anyone else.

Not all know-it-all leaders are so blatant. Some are more indirect, although they still communicate the conviction that they know more about the topic than anyone else, and, therefore, others' opinions do not count for much.

This attitude of superiority, whether blatantly or subtly communicated, tends to create feelings of inferiority among members of the group. As a result, even though the leader may ask for their opinions, the members rarely speak up for fear that their ideas will be of little consequence compared to the superior knowledge of the expert. Thus, a wealth of experiential knowledge that the group may have is lost. Consequently, know-it-all leaders may make decisions based on theories that are not relevant for the local situation, leading to ineffective or even negative outcomes. Furthermore, they often become discouraged, complaining that nobody participates or contributes anything.

The lack of integration between the leader and other group members affects both the unity of the group and the execution of its tasks, while feelings of inferiority within the group keep its members from developing their potential.

MANIPULATIVE LEADERSHIP

Some who practice the previous modes of leadership may be sincere in their desire to help the group or to stimulate its participation, without realizing how their own attitudes of superiority obstruct the group's ability to do so. In contrast, manipulative leaders only pretend to have the well-being of others at heart in order to hide their true motives and personal interests.

People generally respond to this mode of leadership, which is especially common in politics, with disillusionment and mistrust. When people find out they have been manipulated, they become cynical and suspicious. The lingering memory of betrayal damages the spirit of cooperation and makes it very difficult for any organization or project to regain their trust.

In short, manipulative leadership is antithetical to the three group functions because it destroys trust, precludes unity, and seeks to use others, rather than help them develop their potential. While group members may work to accomplish tasks as long as they believe in the leader, as soon as they discover they are being used, they quit.

COMMON DRAWBACKS

Although outwardly there are many differences between these four modes of leadership, in all four the leader attempts to dominate the group by controlling the process of decision-making, whether it be through the force of authority, care, knowledge, or manipulation. In the final analysis, the purpose of maintaining control through domination serves an egotistical need for power. As a result, none of these styles of leadership are effective means for achieving the three primary functions of a group.

All four completely ignore the task of developing the capabilities of group members. Moreover, the reaction that each of these leadership modes provokes in the group tends to destroy the group's belief in its own potential. Resentment and rebelliousness block positive efforts and extinguish the desire for excellence. Dependence paralyzes learning, responsibility and creative initiative. Feelings of inferiority undermine confidence in the members' own knowledge and abilities. Mistrust destroys the foundation of cooperative efforts.

Without unity of thought, a shared vision, and mutual support, it is very difficult for a group to function as an effective team. Authoritarian and know-it-all leaders alienate themselves from group members, thus causing disunity, even though the members may be relatively united among themselves in opposing the leader. Manipulative leaders, because of the distrust they create, not only generate disunity between the group and the leader, but also alienate group members from one another. Paternalistic leaders can foster superficial unity, which may include positive feelings between group members and the parent-leader of the group. Nevertheless, the relationship of dependence and the relative lack of responsibility among members deprive this mode of leadership of the empowering effect of true unity among equals.

All of these modes of leadership usually manage to accomplish the group's tasks to some degree. Indeed, these achievements may even be attributed to the strong direction of the leader. However, this apparent strength is, in reality, a weakness. Leadership by domination, no matter what form it takes, limits the productivity and the quality of the group's achievements because its accomplishments can only reflect the strengths and weaknesses of the leader. The group cannot surpass its leader. The synergy that integrates the contributions and talents of all members depends upon creative interaction among equals. It can never emerge when one person dominates the rest. Likewise, continuity of purpose and perseverance to achieve long-term goals are unlikely, since the members are not nurtured to effectively replace the functions of the leader when it becomes necessary.

In contrast, when leaders encourage group members to share their ideas, participate in the decision-making process, take initiative and shoulder responsibility, the strengths and insights of each member helps to compensate for the weaknesses and misperceptions of the others. This synergistic effect leads the group to greater achievements than any leader-dominated group could hope to attain.

Despite all the shortcomings in the dominant modes of leadership, some people will argue that each of them is appropriate in particular situations. They cite as an example, the need for authoritarian leadership during an emergency, such as a fire. In daily life, however, situations that would justify these modes of leadership are extremely rare. Rather, we could say that each of these styles of leadership has redeeming characteristics that can be salvaged and integrated into a more empowering mode of leadership. Authoritarian leaders are often well organized, with a strong drive to get the work done. Paternalistic leaders often truly care about the members of the group. Know-it-all leaders usually have valuable technical knowledge to contribute. Manipulative leaders, at the very least, have a clear idea of the ends they are pursuing and tend to think strategically about how to achieve those ends.

However, such characteristics do not justify these modes of leadership. Rather, in order for their qualities or knowledge to enhance group functioning, these leaders must undergo a fundamental transformation in their mental model of leadership and develop a host of other concepts, skills, attitudes, and qualities.

We also need to recognize that all of us may succumb to one or more of these leadership modes in our daily lives, switching back and forth between one mode and another depending on circumstances. Thus, we may be authoritarian with our subordinates, paternalistic with our children, and know-it-all with certain colleagues. As we become aware of these tendencies in ourselves and of the circumstances in which we adopt each mode of leadership, we can make a conscious effort to modify our actions.

DEMOCRATIC LEADERSHIP

Those who recognize the need to transform the four previous modes of leadership often vaunt democratic leadership as the solution. Therefore, we will briefly examine the pros and cons of democratic leadership as it is most commonly practiced, to see if it adequately responds to the challenges of our age.

Two distinctive characteristics of democratic leadership are:

1) commitment to an electoral process (representative democracy); and

2) emphasis on participatory processes in decision-making (participatory democracy).

Democratic leaders are elected. They are not arbitrarily chosen by those in power, nor do they impose themselves upon the will of the people, or take power by force of arms. This, in itself, is a significant achievement.

Ideally, democratic leadership encourages decision-making based on participation and the free interchange of ideas. However, the focus of participation can vary. An adversarial model of democracy based on opposition perceives others as foes and leads to debate and confrontation. In contrast, participatory democracy is characterized by dialogue and consensus.

In the ideal scenario — participatory democracy — leaders perceive their role during meetings as that of facilitator, encouraging a search for truth and appreciation for everyone's ideas, as they guide the group towards true consensus. This leads to a creative integration of ideas that results in more effective outcomes than what any one individual could have produced alone.

In order to achieve these results, it is helpful for a leader to:

1) *Inform the group of the purpose of the meeting and process of decision-making:* The leader needs to be transparent about whether the group has the authority to make the final decision or whether he is seeking input to enrich his own thinking but will be making the final decision himself. This clarification avoids confusion and resentment.

2) *Explain the process of finding truth and insuring justice through consultation*: If group members understand that every point of view is necessary to see the larger whole and equitable outcomes depend on it, they will seek solutions that benefit all parties, rather than fighting over personal interests.

3) *Assume the role of facilitator*: A good leader will elicit contributions from every member, listen attentively, and in a spirit of humility, offer his contribution to the overall consultation.

4) *Summarize*: The leader can assist the process of reaching consensus by providing periodic summaries of the different alternatives that have been presented and the possibilities for consensus that have emerged, until a mutually agreeable solution can be reached.

5) *Acknowledge contributions*: The spirit of unity in the group is enhanced when the leader appreciates the other group members for their contributions and for the group's achievements, humbly deflecting credit from himself.

6) *Encourage universal participation*: By involving everyone in the work to be done, opportunities to acquire new knowledge, experiences, and capabilities increase, unity is enhanced and the pace of learning accelerates.

When leaders develop and practice these attitudes and skills, group members enjoy working together because their ideas are considered and their contributions valued. In such groups, the members recognize that developing their capabilities, strengthening group unity and accomplishing tasks are not antagonistic goals, but rather complementary and often mutually reinforcing. Decisions taken through this process are whole-heartedly supported and not likely to be undermined or surreptitiously opposed.

Unfortunately, examples of true participatory democracy are exceedingly rare.

PROBLEMS WITH DEMOCRACY AS COMMONLY PRACTICED

If a poll were taken, we would probably discover that most leaders in almost any kind of organization consider themselves to be democratic. Although there is a positive trend toward democratic leadership, there are several problems with its practice in the world today. For the most part, the mental model of adversarial democracy is the source of these difficulties. Many problems would disappear if we practiced participatory democracy committed to collective well-being.

Some of the most troublesome issues are:

1) The system of electioneering, campaigning, and nominations leads to a lack of suitable candidates.

2) The concept of democracy is narrowly interpreted, focusing on representative democracy and the electoral process, while ignoring the participatory dimension of democracy.

3) Pseudo-participation is common; that is, leaders invite group members to give their opinions, but continue to impose their own ideas.

4) The decision-making process is often based on struggles among partisan interests, negotiation and coalition building — practices that work against the common good.

5) There is little emphasis on other capabilities needed to exercise effective leadership.

The degree to which democratically elected leaders actually represent the will of the people, or of the organization, is often highly questionable. Although all members of an organization, a municipality or a country may have the opportunity to vote in an election, the question remains, "Who chooses the candidates? How are they selected? What criteria predominate when nominating them?"

All too often, not one person on the list of official candidates is truly suitable. The system of nominations, propaganda, and campaigns generally does not favor honest candidates motivated by a spirit of service. Instead, it attracts egocentric candidates motivated by love of power. Commonly, such a candidate vociferously proclaims, "I am the best," raises money from vested interests to which he becomes beholden, and is willing to say or do anything in order to win. These are not the characteristics of leadership needed today to address and resolve the world's pressing problems. The low turnouts in elections and the number of blank ballots cast are symptoms of this problem.

> *The ideology of partisanship that has everywhere boldly assumed democracy's name… today finds itself mired in the cynicism, apathy, and corruption to which it has given rise. In selecting those who are to take collective decisions on its behalf, society does not need and is not well served by the political theater of nominations, candidature, electioneering, and solicitation.*[3]

The solution is not to do away with elections, but rather to experiment with new types of elections, such as "elections without candidates." In this model, voters identify the capabilities and qualities needed for a given position. Then, without discussion of any candidates, they vote by secret ballot for those individuals they personally believe best meet those requirements and who also manifest a spirit of service and commitment to the common good. All members of the organization are candidates in the sense that any of them may be elected. Neither before, during, nor after the election do members comment to one another about for whom they are going to vote, much less electioneer for or against one person or another.

In practice, this type of system tends to result in the election of more capable, service-oriented individuals. Furthermore, it helps to maintain the unity of the organization. When there are no candidates, no one resents not being elected. This facilitates everyone uniting behind those elected, whoever they might be. Although it is easier to carry out elections without candidates in relatively small organizations or communities where everyone knows each other, this method is also practiced in national and international organizations, using a system of delegates chosen through the same method of elections without candidates.

Thus far, we have dealt with "representative democracy," considering the use of different electoral systems for selecting a leader or board to represent a larger group. Now we will turn our attention to the way leadership is exercised after the election, to see if current practices favor true participatory democracy.

Mere representative democracy narrowly interprets democracy to mean, "duly elected." Once elected, however, leaders may be authoritarian, paternalistic, know-it-all, or manipulative. They may feel and act superior to others, hold all decision-making power in their own hands, and seldom consider the opinions of others, even though they may give others the opportunity to express their ideas. In fact, it is not uncommon for those who have been elected to a position of leadership in an organization to suddenly change their way of acting and begin to exercise a dominant mode of leadership, simply because that is their mental model of how leaders should act.

Even if leaders believe participation to be an essential part of democracy, they may only allow other members pseudo-participation, giving them the opportunity to voice their opinions, but paying little or no attention to their ideas when it comes to making decisions. In fact, leaders may even attend meetings having already decided what they are going to do, before consulting with the group members.

In the best of cases, leaders who only permit a semblance of participation may do so out of ignorance, failing to understand true participatory processes and lacking the skills needed to facilitate them. In the worst of cases, they consciously try to manipulate others, seeking to give the appearance of participation, with no real commitment to the process.

Another problem arises when participation is understood as a conflict among irreconcilable positions. In this case, discussion often bogs down in struggles among opposing factions, especially when some members are motivated by personal, party, or sectarian interests rather than by commitment to the common good. Consequently, the group is paralyzed and little is accomplished. This problem is especially common when partisan politics, the struggle for power, and opposing interest groups are seen as necessary elements of democratic practice. In this model of adversarial democracy, leaders not only have to deal with opposing factions, but also are themselves members of a faction and are expected to represent the interests of those who elected them. In response to these expectations, leaders tend to promote narrow partisan interests at all costs, even when the welfare of the whole is jeopardized.

The fact is, however, that we live in an interdependent society in which the well-being of each part contributes to that of the whole, and the well-being of the whole influences that of each part. In the long run, disregard for this interdependence, resulting in shortsighted, selfish decisions, adversely affects everyone involved, including the group that sought to profit from those decisions.

In the light of these considerations, we can conclude that the degree to which democratic leadership contributes to the three group functions depends on the leaders' understanding of democracy. If leaders limit their understanding of democracy to elections and representative democracy, without taking into account its participatory dimension, or if they only allow pseudo-participation, then their impact on group functioning will be that of authoritarian, paternalistic, know-it-all, or manipulative leaders, depending on the model they actually implement once in power. On the other hand, if their concept of democracy also includes true group participation in decision-making, then the degree to which the group accomplishes its tasks and reaches its goals will depend largely on its success in creating group unity. The degree of unity will most likely be inversely proportional to the pernicious influence of factionalism. That is, participatory democracy will achieve much more than adversarial democracy.

With regard to the third group function — that of developing the potentialities of group members — the adversarial democratic model does not motivate leaders to encourage members to develop their capabilities. Participatory democracy, on the other hand, seeks to facilitate the contribution of every member, recognizing that it will redound to the common good. When the more powerful or knowledgeable members help to cultivate the capabilities of all members, everyone benefits.

In conclusion, the model of democratic leadership takes a number of steps in the right direction, but is still incomplete and subject to manipulation and abuse. Exchanging the mental model of adversarial democracy for a conceptual framework of participatory democracy would be a major step towards enhancing democratic functions. Even then, 'democracy' as a model is limited to those who hold formal leadership positions. It ignores the vast majority of people who hold no formal positions yet are capable of exercising leadership in society, contributing to one or another of the group functions.

Furthermore, even if democratic leaders seek the common good, encourage dialogue and consensus, promote unity, and try to develop the capabilities of group members, there are some final questions to consider. Is a commitment to elections and participation enough to ensure the type of leadership that the world needs today? Are not other capabilities essential for effective leadership, such as initiative, perseverance, justice, self-evaluation, vision, a spirit of service, learning through reflection on action, acting with integrity, and even imbuing one's actions with love?

We therefore propose a new conceptual framework that goes beyond democratic leadership and is capable of addressing the challenges of today's world — *transformative leadership* — an approach informed by evidence and ethical principles and based on the development of capabilities. This is an integrative model that seeks to generate a culture of collaboration based on shared moral values, ethical principles and scientific evidence, motivated by the search for truth and for mutually beneficial solutions.

.

CHAPTER IV

A CONCEPTUAL FRAMEWORK OF

TRANSFORMATIVE LEADERSHIP

"Sow a thought, reap an action;

Sow an action, reap a habit;

Sow a habit, reap a character;

Sow a character, reap a destiny."

— Unknown author

NEED FOR A NEW CONCEPTUAL FRAMEWORK OF LEADERSHIP

In Chapter I we looked at the context in which we live and gained a better understanding of the historical and social processes at work. In Chapters II and III we identified and critically analyzed some common mental models in order to understand their limitations and flaws. We have seen that our prevailing understanding of human nature, of society and of leadership have limitations and may even be seriously inaccurate. In fact, we should be feeling very disturbed by the underlying flaws that we now see in assumptions that we have held all our lives about how the world functions.

Critically examining long held beliefs can indeed be painful. Realizing that they are flawed may provoke disturbing feelings of disorientation and anxiety. This is to be expected and is an essential part of the process of personal transformation. It is these feelings of disorientation that can, in fact, create the receptivity needed to consider a new conceptual framework of leadership capable of replacing the mental models that we have found wanting.

Dissatisfaction with our mental models opens the mind to consider alternative perspectives. If we desire to change or transform our behavior, we not only have to question our faulty mental models, we need to replace them with a new conceptual framework. If we do not adopt a conceptual framework that supports the desired transformation, all behavioral changes will be short lived, for in the end, our behavior conforms to our way of thinking.

The next step consists of exploring the elements of the conceptual framework within a supportive environment in order to integrate them into our thinking patterns and become increasingly conscious of their implications for our behavior. Social support and interaction provide the accompaniment we need to "try out" new behaviors and see their effects.

In this chapter, we propose a conceptual framework of transformative leadership. In Part II, we will look at the final step that will give us the tools we need to bring our new understanding into reality — the capabilities necessary for effecting transformation.

Some may object to the proposal of a values-based conceptual framework, questioning, "Whose values are you promoting?" or, "Aren't you imposing your values on other cultures?" It is important to emphasize at this juncture that the principles and values upon which this conceptual framework is based do not belong exclusively to any culture. They are not "owned" by anyone. These are universal values, embraced by all people everywhere. They are not Western or Eastern, Northern or Southern, developed or developing. The artificial barriers that we create to divide people are products of our own minds, our own fragmented ways of thinking and outdated mental models. If we delve into the spiritual heritage of any culture of the world, we will find the same basic values. In 1993, the Parliament of the World's Religions produced a document entitled, "Declaration Toward a Global Ethic," endorsed by over 100 leaders of the worlds religions and spiritual traditions which stated:

> We affirm that a common set of core values is found in the teachings of the religions, and that these form the basis of a global ethic…
>
> We affirm that there is an irrevocable, unconditional norm for all areas of life, for families and communities, for races, nations, and religions. There already exist ancient guidelines for human behavior which are found in the teachings of the religions of the world and which are the condition for a sustainable world order.
>
> We declare: We are interdependent. Each of us depends on the well-being of the whole… All our decisions, actions, and failures to act have consequences.
>
> We must treat others as we wish others to treat us… We consider humankind our family. We must strive to be kind and generous…. We must strive for a just social and economic order, in which everyone has an equal chance to reach full potential as a human being. We must speak and act truthfully and with compassion, dealing fairly with all, and avoiding prejudice and hatred…

We must move beyond the dominance of greed for power, prestige, money, and consumption to make a just and peaceful world…

Earth cannot be changed for the better unless the consciousness of individuals is changed first…. [1]

These values – love, justice, compassion, generosity, charity, honesty, and trustworthiness – resonate with all people everywhere and connect all humanity. It is these values that guide transformative leadership.

Since the elements we propose are related systemically, it is difficult to speak of one without referring to the others. So we begin by listing all six elements of the conceptual framework. We will then explore the importance and implications of each one.

1. *Service-Oriented Leadership*
2. *Purpose of Leadership: Personal and Social Transformation*
3. *Moral Responsibility to Investigate and Apply Truth*
4. *Essential Nobility of Human Beings*
5. *Transcendence*
6. *Development of Capabilities*

SERVICE-ORIENTED LEADERSHIP

The best way to find yourself is to lose yourself in the service of others.

– Mahatma Gandhi

When people are asked what it means to exercise leadership, they often respond, "to be in charge, to give orders, to be in command, to be number one, to be the decision maker." These replies indicate that the egocentric modes of leadership that have often dominated the pages of history regrettably still prevail in the affairs of the world today.

Unfortunately, authoritarian, paternalistic, manipulative, know-it-all and adversarial democratic modes of leadership continue to predominate and cripple the very groups they claim to serve. In all of them, leaders maintain control over the group by consolidating decision-making power in their own hands. In doing so, they can impose their will and ensure that the group serves them. Because this mind-set of leadership is based on an egocentric ambition for power over others, these mental models need to be questioned and replaced by a conceptual framework that can transform this self-serving orientation into an approach that values service to others. Transformative leadership does just that; its fundamental characteristic is the spirit of service to the common good. Those who most *serve* the community, not those who most *dominate* it, exercise true leadership. Transformative leadership transfers power from the individual leader to the group. It is exercised when the members of the group sincerely serve the common good, unlike leadership exercised by a privileged few for their own personal benefit.

Service-oriented leadership has several distinguishing characteristics. If we wish to exercise it, whether from a position of formal authority or simply as a member of the group, we need to:

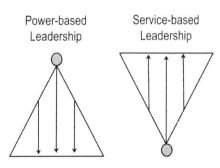

Power-based Leadership

Service-based Leadership

1) consider leadership as an opportunity for service to others, rather than for self-aggrandizement;

2) help others to develop their capabilities, so that they may also exercise leadership;

3) be motivated in our service by love for the people we serve or by devotion to an ideal to which we are committed;

4) demonstrate humility by exercising "invisible leadership," quietly serving the common good, without seeking recognition; and consequently

5) discover the joy of exercising service-oriented leadership.

Prevailing modes of leadership are based on domination using different forms of power. In these modes, leaders consider themselves superior to others in the group. They want to dominate so that the group serves them. In contrast, when we exercise transformative leadership we use our capabilities to serve others and to help them progress. Rather than exalting ourselves, our words and actions are characterized by humility.

We must be careful to distinguish between the spirit of service that characterizes transformative leadership and the pseudo-service of the paternalistic leader, who does for others what they could learn to do for themselves. True service is characterized by wisdom and does not create dependency, but rather frees people from it. It seeks not to bind, but to emancipate. It respects the dignity of each person. Its purpose is to empower those who are served. Therefore, it is not concerned solely with satisfying the immediate needs of the members of the organization or community, but rather with assisting all members to develop the capabilities they need in order to contribute to their own material, intellectual, and spiritual well-being. This will then have ripple effects in their families, organizations, and communities.

A commitment to empowering others implies sensitivity to the capabilities, interests, and potentialities of each person. It signifies giving people the opportunity to learn, inviting them to engage in tasks that may be challenging, but not so overwhelming that they lead to discouragement. At times, it entails supporting others as they carry out a task, even though we could have performed the task faster and more efficiently ourselves. It implies inviting them to participate in activities as "apprentices," so that through participation they learn how to carry out a particular activity themselves. It includes encouraging others to take initiative and then accompanying them as they struggle to acquire the new capabilities needed to reach their goal.

CONSTRUCTING A CATHEDRAL

During the Middle Ages, two workers were carrying very large blocks of stone up a steep slope.

The first man was grumbling and complaining about his hard lot in life. When a passerby asked him what he was doing, he replied brusquely, "Can't you see? I have to lug these heavy stones up the hill to the construction site."

The second man, in spite of the fact that he was bowed under the weight of a stone that was even heavier than that of his companion, seemed happy and joyful. When the passerby asked him what he was doing, he replied, "I'm helping to build a cathedral, in which men will sing praises to the glory of God."

The spirit of service that inspires transformative leadership is born from the recognition and whole-hearted acceptance that our true station in life is that of a servant to humanity, using our unique talents to contribute to a better world. Then, by finding a cause truly worthy of our devotion, service to it becomes a motivating power in our lives.

When you love, you wish to do things for. You wish to sacrifice for. You wish to serve.[2]

– Ernest Hemingway

When we are imbued with the spirit of service, we do not act out of a desire for personal gain, from fear of punishment, or even from a sense of obligation. Rather, we are motivated by love: love for truth, love for humankind, love for God, or more concretely, love for community, love for family, or love for whomever we are serving. When service is motivated by love, it becomes a powerful force that can have a transforming effect both on others and on us.

When we are infused with the spirit of service, we do not ask, "What can the community do for me?" Rather, we ask, "How may I best serve my community?" or better yet, "What service does my community need that I can render?" At times, the most necessary services are not the most exciting, interesting, or prestigious. They may very well be tedious jobs that nobody else wants to do. Nevertheless, once we have discerned the relationship between the needs and the noble ideal we serve, we do not consider any service beneath our rank. Rather, we respond without waiting to be asked.

> ### The Nurse
>
> *During a war, a nurse was working in a military hospital, helping soldiers wounded in battle. One day, a general paid a visit to the hospital to observe the state of things, and was aghast at the awful conditions and the nauseating stench. "I wouldn't do this work for a hundred thousand dollars," he exclaimed. The nurse looked at him and said, "I wouldn't do it for money either."*

An analogy for service-oriented leadership may be found in the relationship between the wind and the sailboat that it propels. Although invisible, the wind is the force that keeps the sailboat moving toward its destination. Transformative leadership is content to remain invisible, while actively striving to act in ways that ensure that individual and collective transformation are progressively moving forward.

The words of Lao Tzu express the goal of invisible leadership: "A leader is best when people barely know he exists; when his work is done, his aim fulfilled, they will say: we did it ourselves." [3]

We must be careful, however, not to misinterpret this saying. It does not mean that the role of leadership is to make people think that they have done something when, in fact, they have not. Such an interpretation could lead to a subtle form of manipulation. Rather, the saying implies that true leadership empowers people to develop and use their capabilities in order to accomplish their goals for themselves, working hand-in-hand with the leader. Invisible leadership implies that we detach ourselves from the expectation of recognition as a reward for our services and that we resist the temptation to magnify our own contributions and to call attention to our role as leader. Invisible leadership requires giving ample credit to those who share in the work, or to the group as a whole.

> *It is amazing what you can accomplish if you do not care who gets the credit.*
>
> *— Attributed to Harry Truman*

If we strive to serve the common good, we will soon discover in this service a source of abiding satisfaction. Although we seek no personal gain or recognition, the desire to serve will motivate us to develop new capabilities that are useful to us in various spheres of life. In this way, service contributes to our own personal transformation. Learning to restrain the ego and to cultivate our higher nature fills us with feelings of dignity and of dominion over our own lives. We feel added pleasure when we see the capabilities that others are developing and the progress that they are making, recognizing that in some way we have contributed to their well-being. The sense of having achieved meaningful objectives in service to a noble purpose enriches our lives with deep inner satisfaction.

AN ELDERLY WOMAN'S SERVICE [4]

An eighty five year old woman was being interviewed on her birthday. "What advice would she have for people her age?" the reporter asked.

"Well," said the old dear, "at our age it is very important to keep using all our potential or it dries up. It is important to be with people and, if it is at all possible to earn one's living through service. That's what keeps us alive and well."

"May I ask what exactly you do for a living at your age?"

"I look after an old lady in my neighborhood," was her unexpected, delightful reply.

PURPOSE OF LEADERSHIP: PERSONAL AND SOCIAL TRANSFORMATION

...The honor and distinction of the individual consist in this, that he among all the world's multitudes should become a source of social good. [5]

– 'Abdu'l-Bahá

When creating a framework for transformative leadership, questions regarding the purpose of human existence are of fundamental importance. The conceptual framework of transformative leadership is based on the conviction that human beings have a dual purpose in life that gives direction and meaning to their existence. The first is to engage in a process of personal transformation, developing qualities

91

and capabilities that perfect us as human beings. The second is to involve ourselves in the process of social transformation, contributing to the advancement of civilization. Recognition and acceptance of this two-fold purpose for existence orients us toward a meaningful life.

The objective of personal transformation is to transform our latent potentialities into a living reality, in which our physical, intellectual, and spiritual dimensions reach continually higher levels of expression. This transformation occurs as we develop qualities and capabilities that reflect our essential nobility. Some of these are generic capabilities, such as the capabilities of transformative leadership that empower our efforts in all fields of endeavor. Others are technical capabilities, related to our unique talents or profession. The development of both types of capabilities gives us a sense of fulfillment and enables us to make increasingly significant contributions to society.

The objective of the complex process of social transformation is to build an ever-advancing civilization based on principles of justice, unity, and love. A social system that is "at once progressive and peaceful, dynamic and harmonious, a system giving free play to individual creativity and initiative but based on cooperation and reciprocity"[6] is indeed a highly complex and challenging task.

Personal transformation and a commitment to social transformation are mutually reinforcing. When personal transformation is not motivated by the desire to contribute to social transformation, we run the risk of self-centeredness, developing our capabilities only for our own personal benefit. Even worse, if we only concentrate on the development of technical capabilities, we may use them to exploit or harm others.

Likewise, a commitment to social transformation alone has its pitfalls. One of the fundamental tasks in the process of social transformation at all levels of society is to convert vertical relationships based on domination, into mutually supportive horizontal relationships. If attempts at social transformation are unaccompanied by personal transformation, the best that can be achieved is limited structural change. However, these changes cannot lead to a just and united society if the protagonists of change are not themselves striving in their daily lives to practice justice and to promote unity through the practice of true leadership. Without personal transformation, the ills that plague the old social structures,

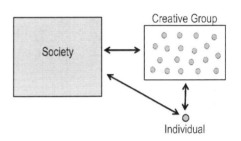

Personal and Social Transformation

such as corruption, nepotism, disunity, prejudice, and discrimination, will also pervade the new, since these ills grow out of the defects of those who work within the structures.

Working simultaneously on both personal and social transformation has a synergistic effect. Each type of transformation stimulates further development of the other. It is not possible to attain personal transformation in a social vacuum. We are all part of a world characterized by increasing interdependence. The path to personal transformation, therefore, is not to be found in living a solitary existence cut off from the rest of the world, but rather through interaction with others. The challenges encountered while working for social transformation require us to develop new capabilities, while our desire to contribute to a better world motivates us to do so. Then, as we develop more capabilities and exercise them more effectively, we are empowered to make ever more significant contributions to social transformation. Thus, our efforts toward personal transformation and social transformation become a virtuous circle, each contributing to the other.

Personal and social transformation are both nurtured through fellowship in a community. Therefore, an organization, or even an informal group of friends, committed to this dual process creates an environment that motivates and sustains us in our efforts. The existing values and customs of society naturally influence our character and behavior. Therefore, in a society where corruption is the norm, a far greater effort is required to practice justice and integrity than in a society where justice and integrity are accepted as the norm. Being members of a group committed to transformation – a micro-society with common ideals – gives us strength to persevere in our personal efforts to develop our capabilities and strengthens our resolve to pursue transcendent goals.

Such a group or organization also helps us to renew our energies and our commitment to promoting change in the larger society. Moreover, the group itself has a much greater potential to influence the direction of change than the sum of its individual members, since it can undertake projects that have a greater impact on society than those tackled by individuals working separately. In short, both types of transformation are most likely to occur when a group of people, however small it may be, works toward those goals.

In an age like ours, there is a great need to form such "creative groups." If we feel we are already part of a creative group, we can strengthen it by introducing its members to the conceptual framework of transformative leadership and consciously committing ourselves to both personal and social transformation. If we do not belong to such a group, we can initiate one by sharing these ideas with friends or colleagues who may be inspired by the possibilities.

The work of personal and social transformation is facilitated when we take into account two basic requirements. First, we need a vision of the ideal toward which we are striving in order to provide direction and focus. Having a vision of an 'ideal human being' guides our personal transformation by providing a standard toward which to strive. The vision of an ideal society awakens our commitment to practice the principles upon which such a society is based, and suggests ways in which we can use our particular strengths to help build a better world. Guided by vision, we can take concrete steps to create a more just, united environment, beginning in our own family and community. A shared vision also contributes to unity of thought in the group, a prerequisite for unity of action.

Without vision, the complex process of social transformation is often understood simply in terms of protest or revolt against the evils of present day society. In contrast, vision provides a clear alternative with which to supplant the existing ills. It is not enough, however, to have an elevated vision based on our cherished ideals and to elaborate a discourse based on that vision. We must also develop the capabilities necessary to implement those ideals in order to transform vision into reality. It is always easier to talk about our vision than to live it. For example, it is easy to emphasize the importance of honesty and upright conduct. It is much more difficult to develop the capability of managing our affairs with integrity.

By studying the elements and capabilities of transformative leadership and striving to practice them, we will develop new ways of thinking and interacting. Individual reflection and group consultation deepen our understanding of the conceptual framework. As a result, our actions become more effective as we strive to serve others by sharing what we have learned and by developing and applying transformative leadership capabilities.

The process of transformation is akin to an ascending, never-ending spiral. No matter how much each person, institution or community progresses, there is always room for improvement. Therefore, the recognition of personal and social transformation as the central purpose of our lives inspires us to strive for noble goals and gives us the courage to persevere.

MORAL RESPONSIBILITY TO INVESTIGATE AND APPLY TRUTH

As we were developing the conceptual framework of transformative leadership, the question arose: what is the basis for the ethical/moral dimension of leadership? We propose that transformative leadership is rooted in our fulfillment of two complementary moral responsibilities:

1) *an unfettered search for truth and the acceptance of those truths that we have verified through our independent investigation,* and

2) *the coherent application, in all aspects of life, of the truths we have accepted.*

In transformative leadership, these twin responsibilities are inseparable. Transformation, by definition, demands action, not just a lofty discourse. Our words must be backed by congruent actions in order for them to be credible. However, not all actions have the same effect. The more fully we understand the reality (truth) of a situation, with all the nuances and principles involved, the greater our possibility for effective action. When we sincerely strive to fulfill these twin moral responsibilities, the light of truth will guide our efforts and serve as a compass for our personal and social transformation.

The ancient and puzzling question then arises: what is truth? Rather than presuming to answer this difficult question, we maintain that each person has the moral responsibility to search for the answer and to live congruently with the conclusions to which his independent investigation leads. What we do affirm is that truth exists, because objective reality exists. For the same reason, truth is one, and not multiple. What is limited and relative is our understanding of truth or reality. Due to our human limitations, we can never come to a full understanding of truth. However, through investigation, we can broaden and deepen our understanding of the truth related to specific aspects of life, and we should strive to do so to the utmost of our ability.

▶ Contingent Truth And Ideal Truth

All our different ways of thinking are to be considered as different ways of looking at the one reality, each with some domain in which it is clear and adequate. One may indeed compare a theory to a particular view of some object. Each view gives only an appearance of the object in some aspect. The whole object is not perceived in any one view but, rather, it is grasped only implicitly as that single reality which is shown in all these views.[7]

– David Bohm

As philosophical discourse throughout the ages attests, there are many ways to think about truth. Two categories of truth concern us deeply in our attempt to practice transformative leadership. The first – *contingent truth* – relates to facts, data and causal relationships "as they are" at a particular moment in time and space. Peter Senge uses the term "current reality" to refer to this category of truth.[8]

It is not an easy task to perceive contingent truth, because our individual backgrounds, habits and mental models limit our perceptions and understanding of facts. Therefore, we need to complement our understanding with the perceptions and understanding of others. As we broaden our knowledge of a particular subject or situation, we will discover that what we had perceived as "truth" in a given moment was only a partial or even an incorrect understanding. Consequently, the investigation of contingent truth implies getting as much information about a situation from as many diverse sources as is reasonably possible before making a judgment and deciding on action.

In everyday situations, investigating contingent truth usually implies seeking out the distinct perspectives of different stakeholders, as a means of broadening our vision and seeing beyond the boundaries of our initial perceptions. This is especially important before making decisions leading to significant changes that will affect others.

The scientific enterprise functions as an institutionalized expression of the investigation of contingent truth. Our understanding of the laws that govern the physical universe, such as the law of gravity, often begins with everyday experience. However, by itself, experience leads to a very limited understanding of these laws in comparison with scientific knowledge. Therefore, in order to gain a deeper understanding of truth about a particular subject matter, we must research scientific evidence that already exists or use scientific methods to expand the boundaries of our knowledge. Even though science provides methods to systematically investigate contingent truth, scientists are the first to admit that their knowledge of truth is relative and not absolute. This humble recognition is what advances knowledge. Similarly, when we speak of the need to investigate truth, it is a relative, but ever-deepening understanding for which we are searching, not absolute understanding.

The second category of truth – *ideal truth* – is concerned with the way "things should be." Ideal truth has to do with principles. In *The Seven Habits of Highly Effective People*, Stephen Covey proposes that there are immutable moral principles that govern human behavior just like there are physical laws that govern the physical universe. This message has resonated so widely that the book has sold over 25 million copies in 40 languages worldwide. Covey further explores this theme in a business context in *Principle-Centered Leadership*, emphasizing that effective leadership is guided by such principles: "Our effectiveness is predicated upon certain inviolate principles – natural laws in the human dimension that are just as real, just as unchanging, as laws such as gravity are in the physical dimension. These principles are woven into the fabric of every civilized society and constitute the roots of every family and institution that has endured and prospered."[9]

These immutable principles are grounded in reality and function in the interpersonal and social realm with the same predictability that physical laws function in the physical world. Since these principles are an integral part of reality, open-minded investigation can lead to their discovery. Therefore, we have the moral responsibility of investigating ideal truth, trying to identify for ourselves those universal principles by which we can guide our actions in the processes of personal and social transformation – principles that, by definition, contribute to the common good.

Just as reflection on everyday experience can help us to discover to a limited degree some basic scientific laws, it can also help us to become aware of some of the spiritual and social principles that govern human life and relationships. Furthermore, just as science embodies the institutionalized expression of the investigation of contingent truth, the world's religions and spiritual traditions serve as the institutionalized expression of humanity's concern with ideal truth. As such, the sacred writings at the heart of all the world's cultures provide a far more comprehensive knowledge of the spiritual and social principles that serve as the moral foundation of civilization than we can deduce on our own. The essential principles these writings emphasize are similar, nurturing throughout history the vision of a just, united, and peaceful world.

Since ethical principles must guide not only personal transformation, but also social transformation, the challenge facing transformative leadership at this critical juncture in history is to build universal consensus on a set of principles that can serve as a moral code for constructing a global society. Both *The Declaration of Human Rights* of the United Nations and the *Declaration Toward a Global Ethic* issued by the Parliament of the World's Religions are examples of documents that attempt to meet that challenge, by setting forth a set of shared social principles that serve as the basis for fostering and nurturing human dignity and humankind's collective well-being throughout the world. Other documents that have resulted from global discourse and carry signatories from many nations exemplify the move toward global consensus on the underlying principles that are to govern human affairs in an increasingly interdependent world.

To summarize, in the process of transformation, we must give equal importance to the investigation of contingent truth (how things currently are) and ideal truth (the principles upon which we construct our vision and guide our actions). Since contingent truth and ideal truth are complementary, without an adequate understanding of one or the other, our understanding of reality is incomplete.

▶ PROCESS OF INVESTIGATING TRUTH

The awareness that we can always come to a deeper comprehension of truth helps us maintain an attitude of humility toward our own acquired knowledge. This desire manifests itself in curiosity, interest in the ideas of others, and a sincere attempt to understand viewpoints different from our own, whatever their source may be.

When we feel ourselves to be "experts" in some field, or simply better educated than others, we often tend to reject their ideas without giving them due consideration. However, if we are committed to the investigation of truth, we will be open to learning from anyone. Often the remarks of a child, or someone with little formal education, or a layperson, may provide a fresh viewpoint that leads to greater understanding. It is not so much that we adopt the totality of that person's ideas, but rather, the interaction of ideas leads us to new insights. As a result, we neither blindly accept the ideas of others, no matter what authority expounds them, nor do we automatically reject them.

> *Buddha says, "Monks and scholars should not accept my words out of respect, but should analyze them as a goldsmith analyzes gold, by cutting, melting, scraping, and rubbing it."* [10]
>
> *— Anthony de Mello*

The responsibility of investigating truth implies that we detach ourselves from second-hand truths that we receive from others. Rather, we strive to see with our own eyes and to know with our own knowledge by analyzing and evaluating the information we receive in the light of scientific evidence and the moral and ethical principles we have embraced. Then, whether we accept the new idea completely, accept it partially, reserve judgment, or reject it, we will be able to give a coherent explanation supporting our action.

Group consultation facilitates this process of analyzing and evaluating ideas, when all participants share what they have perceived and the reasoning behind their views. This allows us to compare our own process of analysis and evaluation with that of others, and to consider lines of reasoning that may not have occurred to us previously. However, in the final analysis, each of us has the moral responsibility of drawing our own conclusions.

The sincere search for truth also requires that we consciously make efforts to free our minds and hearts from any form of prejudice. Prejudice obstructs the perception of truth because it predisposes us to automatically accept or reject certain ideas, without objectively analyzing them. However, truth can only be recognized through impartial assessment.

In addition to investigating the truth about objective reality through critical analysis of ideas acquired from books, conferences, academic programs, or personal conversations, we need to investigate the truth related to our subjective reality by paying attention to our emotional reactions. Feeling hurt, over-reacting, freezing up, and becoming defensive are all indicators that point to sensitive areas – areas in which it is difficult for us to see our actions and ourselves objectively.

First, we must recognize that emotional reactions have meaning and need to be analyzed. Once we calm down, we can try to understand why we react emotionally in certain circumstances, with specific people, or to particular topics. We can then evaluate whether our responses are appropriate and, if not, decide on more effective courses of action. This will lead to greater self-knowledge and progress in our personal transformation.

Interpreting the problems in our lives and the negative emotions they generate as opportunities for learning is not easy. Usually we react to problems by devising quick fixes that temporarily alleviate our discomfort and allow us to get on with life as usual. However, when we have not discovered and dealt with the underlying causes, which often lie within us, the problems reappear later, often in more severe forms.

Engaging in self-examination and wrestling with a problem over time involves living with a level of tension outside our comfort zone. However, when we consider what the problem may be revealing about ourselves, modify our attitudes and actions, and make changes that reflect a deeper understanding of our contributing role, we are more likely to devise long-lasting solutions that address the root causes and not just the symptoms of the problem.

▶ Process of Applying Truth

Since we each have the moral responsibility of investigating truth, no one has the right to tell us what we should believe or what principles we should accept, although others can courteously explain their points of view and ask us to consider them. The corollary of this principle is that we each have the moral responsibility of wholeheartedly striving to practice those principles that we have freely accepted.

If we discover serious inconsistencies between our words and our actions, we have the responsibility of trying to understand the reasons why. We may be ignorant of some essential truths due to deficiencies in carrying out the first moral responsibility of investigating the truth. Alternatively, we may be failing to carry out the second moral responsibility and not applying certain truths we have recognized on a theoretical level. If we discover that we are not fully convinced of the truth and the benefit of applying a principle that we promulgate, we should identify our specific doubts and return to the process of investigation of truth in order to clarify our thinking. However, if we conclude that the principle in question is true, we need to try to understand our behavior and the reasons why we are not 'practicing what we preach.' Then, we can take action — such as meditating on readings related to the principle, identifying concrete situations where we can practice the principle, setting goals for ourselves, and evaluating our progress daily — until our words and deeds become increasingly aligned.

No matter what the cause, the failure to live in harmony with ideal truth will generate problems in our lives, even though we may blame the problems on others or attribute them to bad luck or fate. Moral laws and social principles from the realm of ideal truth generate cause and effect relationships, just as do natural laws that govern the physical universe. If a young child who is not yet cognizant of the law of gravity climbs onto the roof of his house and jumps off in an attempt to fly, he will get hurt. His ignorance of the law does not protect him from its consequences. Similarly, if we are ignorant of fundamental spiritual laws and social principles, we may often feel dissatisfied with life and get hurt in our relationships with others without understanding why.

It is not necessary to understand all the implications of a principle in order to begin practicing it. Based on the understanding that we have attained, we have the responsibility to apply the principle as best we can in our individual and collective lives, while continuing to search for an even fuller understanding. Consistently striving to apply a principle sensitizes us to other implications and stimulates further reflection and investigation. Consequently, the investigation and application of truth play complementary roles in an on-going process of learning.

As we progressively apply in our lives the principles we have accepted, our lives become increasingly *coherent*. Our actions exemplify our words and we are able to explain why we think and act as we do. The outcome is ever greater self-knowledge and tranquility. The fact that both our words and actions are grounded in reality (to the degree that we have been able to understand it) reinforces feelings of self-mastery and contributes to authentic relationships with others.

▶ RELATIONSHIP BETWEEN CONTINGENT AND IDEAL TRUTH

> *The human enterprise is, then, the never ending investigation of reality, the search for truth, the quest for knowledge, and as important, the application of knowledge to achieve progress, the betterment of the world, and the prosperity of its peoples.*[11]
>
> – *Paul Lample*

The physical laws that are discovered through the investigation of contingent truth and the spiritual laws and social principles that are discovered through the investigation of ideal truth are complementary aspects of reality. The investigation of truth requires effort to discover the truth found in both spheres of knowledge, for without one or the other, our understanding of reality is incomplete.

Social transformation and the advancement of civilization also depend on the application of both kinds of truths. Scientific truth provides the practical means by which a materially prosperous civilization can be created. Spiritual truth delineates the principles necessary for the creation of a just, peaceful society – one in which material prosperity is equitably distributed and the limitless potentialities latent in human consciousness are cultivated, rather than one in which material prosperity becomes an end in itself.

The need to identify both contingent truth and ideal truth is also vital for transformation even on a small scale. In practical terms, if we are trying to decide what to do or are searching for a solution to a problem, we need to ascertain the facts, so that we can perceive the current situation from all relevant perspectives as dispassionately as possible. We also need to identify the principles that will lead us to a just solution and formulate a principle-based vision toward which to strive.

Once we have investigated the facts, identified relevant principles, and formulated our vision, we can reflect on the concrete steps necessary to move from current reality toward the vision. Having a clear idea of our final goal will give us an objective criterion with which to evaluate suggested courses of action. Understanding the reality of our current situation can save us from blindly copying strategies that were successful elsewhere. Rather, we can learn from other people's success as well as our own reflection in order to adapt the learning to our situation.

In simple situations, we can sometimes foresee the whole process that will take us from current reality to the ideal reality, with all of the intermediate steps. In more complex situations, the understanding of the relationship between the contingent and the ideal may only give us an idea of the direction to take and of the first steps on our journey. In all cases, raising the problem-solving process to the level of principle generates the commitment required to implement the decisions made.

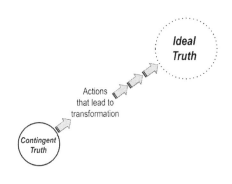

Although we can apply this process as individuals, it is even more fruitful when a group or organization uses it in making plans or resolving problems. In these cases, the ideas expressed by different members will usually include diverse perspectives that can broaden the group's understanding of both the contingent and ideal truth of the situation. Once the group has reached consensus on the most relevant principles, has formulated a vision based on those principles and has developed an understanding of current reality, consultation on possible lines of action will produce a rich variety of ideas. These can then be integrated into a plan that is more complete and effective than any that an individual alone could generate.

▶ Defining Moral Responsibility as Investigation and Application of Truth

When people think of morality they often think of a list of attributes that a moral person should have: truthfulness, honesty, courtesy, forgiveness, and many more. Why do we define moral responsibility in such a different way? Identifying a small number of principles in which we deeply believe, rather than referring to a long list of moral qualities, helps us to remain conscious of those principles and of our commitment to applying them. Viewing the *commitment to truth as our primary moral responsibility* removes the judgmental aspects of the word "morality" — a highly charged word to which some may respond defensively. When we each identify the principles that will guide us, we have greater motivation for applying them than if an outside authority imposed the same principles. It paves the way for self-discipline, rather than external discipline.

Finally, we each apply principles as we understand them. As we practice those principles to which we are committed, our understanding of them deepens and we begin applying them more coherently in different aspects of our lives. We discover how the practice of one principle leads to the practice of other related principles. In this way, an ongoing learning process grounded in the investigation and application of ideal truth helps each person to develop a meaningful and ever-expanding array of qualities and capacities to meet the challenges of life. The result is authentic alignment of actions with truth. This definition of morality implies a proactive outward manifestation of inner development.

ESSENTIAL NOBILITY OF HUMAN BEINGS

> *Mencius said, "First build the nobler part of your nature and then the inferior part cannot overcome it." It is because people fail to build up the nobler part of their nature that it is overcome by the inferior part. In consequence they violate principle...*[12]
>
> *– Lu Hsiang-Shan*

We will only be motivated to strive, and even sacrifice, to create a better world if we believe that it is possible to bring such a world into being, however gradually. This conviction is initiated through the process of critical analysis of flawed mental models of human nature and society, culminating in a new understanding of the essential nobility of each human being. Such a conviction fully recognizes the double nature of man. In no way is it a naive belief in human goodness that ignores the very real atrocities that have been committed throughout history. Rather, it is a belief in human *potential*, combined with the recognition that qualities and capabilities come into being gradually, through appropriate processes of learning and transformation. We find support for this perspective in both the social sciences and in spiritual teachings.

Humanistic psychology and the therapies that have evolved from it, such as *client-centered therapy* developed by Carl Rogers,[13] emphasize the innate tendency toward growth in the core of each human being. The growth can be liberated through a relationship characterized by unconditional acceptance, empathy, and congruence (authenticity). This nurturing relationship creates a safe environment for investigating the truth about one's life, leading to insights concerning unhealthy patterns of action, and resulting in conscious decisions to change – a process contributing to personal transformation.

In more recent years, *positive psychology*, pioneered by Martin Seligman, has gained increasing popularity as a means of enhancing well-being by developing the individual's strengths and latent capacities rather than focusing on weaknesses and maladaptive behaviors. Its aim is to release human potential by cultivating virtues in order to achieve authentic happiness.

Cognitive behavioral therapy (CBT) has demonstrated its effectiveness in a randomized controlled trial.[14] It is now recognized to be a powerful method of helping patients to cope by utilizing the process of transformative learning that we have outlined – examination of faulty beliefs through systematic investigation of truth, their replacement with understandings more aligned with reality, and focused action to develop healthier patterns of behavior. Such a change in understanding, followed by action, engages patients in a process of healing and transformation that nurtures their inherent nobility.

Religious scriptures teach that we have been created in the "image and likeness of God" — that is, we have the *potential* to develop those qualities that are reflections of the attributes of the Divine. One central purpose of life, then, is to develop qualities such as love, forgiveness, truthfulness, uprightness, and justice, with which every human being is potentially endowed.

Both the religious and the psychological approaches emphasize the exercise of free will, the ability we have as human beings to choose our actions, a characteristic that distinguishes man from the rest of creation. Since we have a lower nature (the potential to do evil), as well as a higher nature (the potential to develop noble qualities), we need to consciously choose thoughts and actions that strengthen our higher nature and avoid those that stimulate our lower nature. By focusing on our higher nature, we emphasize the development of noble attributes, such as unity, rather than simply the control or avoidance of defects, such as disunity. Just as light eliminates darkness, the development of positive qualities gradually eliminates defects.

Belief in our essential nobility implies that we strive to develop our own qualities and have faith in the potential nobility of others. We seek a deeper understanding of how to do so through investigating spiritual truths, exploring human potential, and developing a deeper awareness of our own selves. We actively try to perceive others' noble qualities no matter how hidden they may be, and have confidence that they can develop their capabilities, recognize the truth of spiritual principles and respond to a vision based on noble ideals. Through genuine friendship, an inspiring example and a clearly stated vision, we strive to mutually support one another in our efforts to learn and improve.

Both the religious and the secular approaches to the essential nobility of the human being emphasize the process of personal transformation, and of helping others in this process. The religious approach, when it is committed to the establishment of unity, justice and peace in society, also contributes to the process of social transformation. However, in order to properly practice this element of transformative leadership, we need to avoid some erroneous interpretations. A danger in the secular approach is the tendency to become obsessed with personal growth, ignoring the progress and welfare of others. A danger in the religious approach is failing to fully recognize our dual nature, either ignoring our weaknesses and susceptibility to error, or failing to appreciate our innate capacity for nobility.

If we under-estimate the strength of our lower nature, when we commit an error, especially a major one, we may experience deep-seated feelings of unworthiness that cause us to give up on ourselves, rather than using the situation as a learning opportunity that motives us to continue striving. Worse yet, if those around us assume that we should have had the strength to avoid the error, we are likely to rationalize our errors and to hide them from others. If that becomes impossible, we may go to great lengths to avoid those whom we feel may judge us. However, we cannot overcome faults or weaknesses until we recognize and face them. Consequently, denying or minimizing our faults leads to stagnation in our process of transformation.

Conversely, if we are relatively capable of living up to our ideals and do not commit major errors, we face another danger: self-righteousness. We may fall into the trap of considering ourselves to be relatively perfect and take a judgmental attitude toward those who cannot live up to our standards. This attitude impedes not only the growth of others, but also our own. Rather, we need to humbly recognize our own imperfections, focus on those qualities we wish to develop, and remember that we are all at different places on the same path towards realizing our potential nobility.

Embracing the conviction of the essential nobility of human beings also gives us patience and perspective concerning our collective development. It gives us power to see beyond the problems that currently afflict society and the defects of those who generate them. It inspires us to practice transformative leadership, striving to develop our own qualities and capabilities as we work to establish a just, united society.

TRANSCENDENCE

Applying the conceptual framework of transformative leadership is not easy. We are challenged to engage in a constant investigation of truth, to develop and practice self-discipline, to participate in an ongoing learning process, to look for and nurture hidden talents and undeveloped qualities in others, to distinguish ourselves by an attitude of service, to serve the common good, and to strive for the transformation of society. That is a tall order! Yet, anything less would be unworthy of being called *transformative* leadership.

The inspiration to persevere resolutely in this challenging path comes from *transcendence*. When we face obstacles in our path, transcendence gives us strength to continue. We experience transcendence when we detach ourselves from the limitations of current reality and connect with a higher power, or with those eternal values and principles to which we are committed. This inclination to reach toward a higher reality is an inherent aspect of human nature.

▶ Benefits of Transcendence

Transcendence plays a key role in the process of transformation. It keeps us from drowning in a mere glass of water when problems threaten to overwhelm us. When we are frustrated and lost in a forest of details, transcendence enables us to detach from the immediate problem, and, inspired by our vision, to see the whole picture from a broader, more objective vantage point, resulting in a deeper understanding of the dynamics of the situation. Just as a knowledgeable spectator in the stands often grasps the complex dynamics of what is happening on the playing field better than the players who are immersed in the action, transcendence gives us a more comprehensive perspective.

Accepting the moral responsibility to investigate and apply truth implies that we attempt to live by the principles that we have accepted as true, even when those actions run counter to our own self-serving interests. By connecting us with a higher dimension, transcendence gives us the strength to carry out this moral responsibility, to oppose our ego, and to remain steadfast in our efforts to live in accordance with our principles.

Transcendence also helps us keep in touch with those principles during the decision-making process and to use them as a source of insight and guidance. This aspect of transcendence is especially important in group consultation. Raising consultation to the level of principle helps us relinquish our own personal interests and welfare and to consider instead those strategies and lines of action that harmonize with the principles of unity, justice and service to the common good.

In short, transcendence has the effect of renewing and strengthening our commitment so that we can return to problematic situations with a broader perspective, renewed vigor, and moral strength that empowers us to carry on with our work. Then we are able to make decisions and take actions guided by principle.

▶ Methods for Achieving Transcendence

How do we achieve this valuable state of transcendence? One way is through a firm commitment to base our decisions and actions on those principles and values that we have accepted as enduring truths. This commitment connects us with universal principles and gives us strength to overcome the temptation to engage in self-serving activities. Another means of achieving transcendence is through committing to a vision. A vision based on the principles and values we try to live by serves as a source of inspiration for our daily labors. The importance of vision was noted thousands of years ago by King Solomon when he observed that: "Where there is no vision, the people perish."[15] Vision enshrines the hope that life can and will be better. It provides a goal that inspires effort and sacrifice. When we see how our daily labors fit into a larger vision, our work takes on greater meaning.

When principles and values that we have accepted as enduring truths are embodied in the form of a vision — an image of a desired future — that vision will be particularly inspiring and can keep us going in the midst of difficult circumstances. For example, a commitment to the conceptual framework of transformative leadership can be embodied in a vision of an organization or community that is harmonious, equitable, and prosperous. Then, that vision serves as a guiding light in our efforts to transform the organization or community.

On a wider scale, the complex and highly interdependent global community we inhabit also needs a principle-based vision to guide us in the development of a planetary society. According to John W. Gardner, former United States Secretary of Health, Education and

Welfare, and educational advisor to several presidents, "A vision relevant for us today will build on values deeply embedded in human history and in our own tradition. The materials of which we build the vision will be the moral strivings of the species, today and in the distant past."[16]

A shared vision that can be accepted by all people must also incorporate new universal principles. With such a shared vision, humanity could address, from the standpoint of moral principle, the current problems plaguing the planet. As Peter Russell has outlined, the vision needed is "one that is holistic, non-exploitative, ecologically sound, long term, global, peaceful, humane, and cooperative. This would mean a shift to a truly global perspective, one in which the individual, the society, and the planet are all given full recognition."[17]

> *Look deep into nature and then you will understand everything better.*
>
> *— Albert Einstein*

When we are true to our principles and follow a vision, these serve as bearings that keep us oriented. In moments of conflict, confusion and emotional turmoil, however, we may feel the need to do something more concrete that will help us detach from the immediate situation and connect with our principles and vision. If we have religious convictions, prayer, meditation, and reading the sacred writings of our faith are often effective means. Other methods include: communing with nature, relaxation practices, listening to music, reading poetry or inspiring texts, contemplating works of art that express values and principles similar to our own, or consulting with a person who has greater vision or wisdom than we do.

Once achieved, transcendence allows us to see the immediate situation in the light of our vision and principles. The urge to act impulsively is dampened, and we are empowered to act in harmony with our convictions.

In brief, transcendence is a critical element in the framework of transformative leadership and is a necessary practice in the creation of a peaceful world. The problems undermining the foundations of society must necessarily continue to worsen as long as the groups and individuals involved continue to pursue their own selfish benefits and personal interests. Therefore, in striving to resolve these problems, we must recognize the imperative of adhering in all matters to principles that promote the common good. Then, through the practice of transcendence, we acquire the needed strength to rise above our personal concerns and fully commit to discovering and applying principles that are relevant to the problems at hand and coherent with our vision of a better world. Only then can real progress be achieved. It is the challenging task of transformative leadership to facilitate this process and to encourage others to participate in it.

DEVELOPMENT OF CAPABILITIES

Trustworthiness is based on character, what you are as a person and competence, what you can do. If you have faith in my character but not in my competence, you still would not trust me... Without character and competence, we won't be considered trustworthy, nor will we show much wisdom in our choices and decisions.[18]

— Stephen Covey

The development of transformative leadership capabilities is what supplies us with the tools to put into action our transformed perspective. We see the world differently now. Having recognized the flaws in our thinking and our dysfunctional mental models, we can no longer view the world and our place in it the same way. We see the daunting task before us and we need new tools to bring our new understanding into reality.

We understand that transformative leadership not only implies a new concept of leadership, but also requires a new definition of what it means to be an ethical or moral person. Historically, a moral person has been defined in passive terms as a good citizen who accepts and upholds traditional values, and who avoids making waves by challenging the system or trying to change things. Those who advocated social change, such as giving women the right to vote, for example, were considered immoral and a threat to the status quo.

A passive definition of morality no longer meets the needs of our age; rather the crisis of our times compels us to redefine morality in active terms, to shift from what a moral person *is*, to what a moral person *does*. In today's world, to be a moral person is to be a social actor, someone who is consciously and actively engaged in service. To exercise transformative leadership effectively, we need to develop the capabilities that enable and empower us to contribute to the common good.

Before looking at specific capabilities, we need to understand the construct of a "capability." During the course of developing our ideas, when we studied the lives of individuals who have provided examples of transformative leadership in society, we noticed that certain common actions and activities made their leadership effective. When we looked more deeply, we realized that these actions and activities were possible because those performing them possessed a number of basic capabilities. To date, we have identified 18 of these transformative leadership capabilities. While we recognize that this is not a definitive list, we feel that these initial 18 capabilities are highly relevant to the age in which we live.

As we examined these capabilities, we discovered that each one consists of the integration of four types of components – *concepts, skills, attitudes,* and *qualities.* As we progressively acquire and improve our mastery of the concepts, skills, attitudes, and qualities that make up a specific capability, we become empowered to perform those actions and activities that are generated and sustained by that specific capability. Not until the components of a specific capability are properly developed and integrated will we be empowered to exercise the capability effectively.

> *The attainment of any object is conditioned upon knowledge, volition and action... Mere knowledge of principles is not enough.*[19]
>
> — 'Abdu'l-Bahá

All purposeful activity is based on a sequential dynamic of knowledge, will, and action. Since knowledge is the first step in this dynamic, we begin to develop a capability by understanding the relevant concepts and formulating an image of what the capability looks like in practice. This understanding provides a yardstick, or standard, by which to evaluate our progress as we progressively develop the necessary skills, attitudes and qualities.

What follows is a brief description of each of the four components of a capability, complementing the description with examples taken from the capability of "effective group consultation" in decision-making.

Concepts: To practice a capability, we need to understand its key concepts. For example, the capability of "effective group consultation" subsumes the following concepts: the purpose of consultation, the need for diverse views in finding truth, the relationship between consultation and justice, principles underlying effective consultation, the need for unity, qualities required, and steps in effective decision-making. Furthermore, we need a certain degree of understanding of basic concepts related to the issue under consultation.

Skills: Skills are the mechanical or functional abilities needed to implement a capability. For example, listening with empathy, eliciting diverse points of view, creating a safe environment for people to express their thoughts fully, and summarizing ideas, are some of the skills that contribute to the effective practice of consultation.

Attitudes: Attitudes refer to the affective aspect of capabilities. They may be considered as habitual patterns of emotional response. Examples relevant to consultation include curiosity, appreciation, tolerance for ambiguity, and openness to new ideas.

Qualities: The virtues that are reflected in ideal human behavior can be referred to as qualities. Examples of qualities include honesty, patience, kindness, steadfastness, purity, truthfulness, courtesy and trustworthiness. Qualities are simultaneously the foundation of human character and the ideals that guide our efforts. It is not enough, however, to *believe* in these qualities; we must *practice* them in our lives as well. We only exemplify a quality when it is reflected in our patterns of action, whether these are habits or carefully thought-out efforts. If we are to exercise a capability effectively, the importance of practicing the appropriate qualities cannot be overemphasized. For instance, it is impossible to practice the capability of consultation effectively without the qualities of truthfulness and courtesy.

It is sometimes difficult to distinguish between attitudes and qualities because they are closely related. Consider how some might label respect for others and humility as attitudes, while others might define them as qualities. Our goal is not to split hairs in categorization but to motivate the development and practice of the various components that make up a capability.

Once we grasp the concepts involved and have an image of what the capability looks like in action, we can begin to practice it on a rudimentary level. Our degree of proficiency will increase as we progressively acquire the remaining components — skills, attitudes and qualities. As we deal successfully with challenges that require our effective practice of these components, they become increasingly available to us in the acquisition of other capabilities.

While the basic concepts embedded in a capability can be learned fairly rapidly, mastering the needed skills, attitudes and qualities takes time and practice. In fact, these components of the capability can always be developed to a higher degree of perfection. Keeping this in mind helps us to avoid pride and complacency about having mastered a capability just because we can talk about it knowledgeably and are practicing it to some degree. Rather, we will remain humbly aware of the deficiencies in our skills, attitudes and qualities, be open to deeper understanding of the concepts involved, and be receptive to feedback as we struggle to improve. Knowing that progress comes from persistent and faithful effort, we will constantly work to better our mastery of all the components involved.

The development of capabilities is intimately related to the other five elements of the conceptual framework of transformative leadership:

1) A commitment to *personal and social transformation* provides motivation to acquire and utilize capabilities. Conversely, the very act of developing a capability contributes to personal transformation.

2) Our ability to *serve* and contribute to social transformation increases as we develop and refine our practice of a growing number of capabilities.

3) The *investigation and application of truth* gives us criteria for making moral choices as we decide how to use our capabilities.

4) The conviction of our own *essential nobility* gives us confidence in our inherent potential, which is gradually manifested as we develop capabilities.

5) *Transcendence* empowers us to relinquish our egotistical tendencies and to maintain an attitude of humility as we improve. It also helps us to acquire clarity of vision that can guide us as we use our capabilities to face challenges.

The eighteen capabilities of transformative leadership identified to date are listed below. In Part II, we will explore each one briefly. The capabilities are closely interrelated. Consequently, the list is not indicative of any particular order in which they must be mastered. We have, however, divided the capabilities into four groups: capabilities that contribute to personal transformation, capabilities that better interpersonal relationships, capabilities that contribute to social transformation and also an integrative capability. To a certain degree, the capabilities related to personal transformation and to bettering interpersonal relationships are the foundation for the capabilities related to social transformation. However, many of the capabilities affect more than one process.

We have classified "Transformative Leadership in the Family" as an integrative capability. This capability ties all the others together, for it is in the safe haven of the family that we have an invaluable opportunity to develop and practice all the capabilities of transformative leadership.

▶ CAPABILITIES FOR PERSONAL TRANSFORMATION

1. Self Evaluation
2. Learning from Reflection on Action
3. Systemic Thinking
4. Creative Initiative
5. Perseverance
6. Self-Discipline
7. Rectitude of Conduct

▶ CAPABILITIES FOR TRANSFORMATION OF INTERPERSONAL RELATIONS

1. Imbuing Thoughts and Actions with Love
2. Encouragement
3. Effective Group Consultation
4. Promoting Unity in Diversity

▶ CAPABILITIES FOR SOCIAL TRANSFORMATION

1. Establishing Justice
2. Transforming Dominating Relationships

3.   Empowering Education

4.   Elaborating a Principle-Based, Shared Vision

5.   Transforming Institutions

6.   Understanding Historical Perspective

▶ INTEGRATING THE CAPABILITIES

Transformative Leadership in the Family

The conceptual framework of transformative leadership is neither final nor definitive, but evolving. It is this final pillar of the framework — development of capabilities — that initiates an ongoing iterative learning process based on consultation-action-reflection. As a growing number of people and groups consult on the elements of the framework, attempt to apply those elements individually and collectively, and then share their achievements and difficulties, our common understanding of the framework will expand and evolve.

A process of consultation-action-reflection has three characteristics that make it especially appropriate for our work in developing a conceptual framework for transformative leadership suitable for today's world: it focuses on *action*, is *evolving*, and is *participatory*. It is directed toward action and learning, making it compatible with the dual purpose of personal and social transformation. Far from simplifying complex social realities into theoretical constructs confined to the arena of words or intellectual discussions, the consultation-action-reflection process is aimed at generating knowledge relevant to specific situations that contribute to individual and collective transformation.

Although the conceptual framework of transformative leadership is both internally coherent as well as consistent with our life experiences, we recognize that it must evolve. The dynamism of consultation-action-reflection implies that as participants in transformative leadership engage in iterations of this learning process, continual improvement will naturally occur as learning is incorporated. These changes, in turn, will generate new questions, ideas, and fresh alternatives that will be considered in further consultation and application.

We have seen from experience that transformative leadership has universal validity and is successfully practiced in different cultural and national settings. These diverse experiences naturally contribute to a growing understanding of the concepts implicit in each element and capability of transformative leadership and to the continual improvement of methods and materials.

PART II

DEVELOPING

CAPABILITIES

CHAPTER V

CAPABILITIES FOR

PERSONAL TRANSFORMATION

SELF-EVALUATION

Self-knowledge and a commitment to personal transformation are indispensable in our efforts to contribute to a better world. Without this personal commitment, efforts to achieve structural changes that can transform current systems into ones that are just and transparent cannot succeed. Personal and social transformation occur simultaneously. Therefore, our journey begins with a commitment to personal transformation.

Self-evaluation is indispensable for personal transformation because it helps us recognize our strengths and weaknesses and become proactive in striving for excellence. Based on this knowledge, we can choose fields of service where we may best use our talents in service to others and maximize our own learning. We can also develop strategies to strengthen areas in which we are weak. Knowledge of our weaknesses motivates teamwork, leading us to seek collaboration with those whose strengths complement ours. By doing so, we prevent our weaknesses from obstructing progress.

Self-evaluation can make us feel vulnerable. It is unpleasant to acknowledge our weaknesses and challenging to develop the strengths we need to overcome our flaws. Consequently, we often avoid self-evaluation. If we do attempt it, ego — that part of us that single-mindedly pursues self-interest — often blinds us. Our ego justifies our mistakes, reassures us that there are valid reasons to be as we are, comforts us with the thought that 'compared to others we are doing very well,' and usually convinces us that we do not need to change. However, it is not with *others* that we need to compare ourselves, but rather, with the highest criteria of *excellence* that we can imagine. When these criteria are personified by an example of an outstanding human being or are organized in a coherent structure of ideals, they can be powerful guides for growth. *Transformative leadership* is one such framework of coherently organized criteria that serves as an ideal towards which we can strive.

Self-evaluation demands we hold ourselves accountable for our actions. However, it can be overwhelming to continually compare ourselves with a standard of perfection in all things. It will be less daunting to achieve growth by focusing on one or two capabilities of transformative leadership at a time. We may even decide to concentrate on isolated skills, attitudes, or qualities that, when combined with others, form a capability.

▶ SYSTEMATIC APPROACH TO EVALUATING A CAPABILITY

1) *Understand both its visible and invisible dimensions*: We must fully comprehend the *concepts, skills, attitudes and qualities* that

make up the capability: For example, if we wish to create more harmonious, mutually supportive relationships, we need to:

- understand the implications of *mutuality, cooperation, collaboration, service* and *justice*;

- develop skills in *empathetic listening, delegating* and *integrating diverse ideas*;

- demonstrate an attitude of *humility, appreciation,* and *love*; and

- show forth qualities of *truthfulness, trustworthiness, selflessness,* and *kindness*.

2) *Reflect on our actions to evaluate the degree to which we have developed each of these components:* When we reflect on our actions, we often focus on our weaknesses and errors. This leads to feelings of worthlessness and hopelessness. Instead, this can be a positive exercise of:

- *Learning*: The aim of self-reflection is not to engage in self-flagellation; the purpose is to *learn*. We want to measure progress. This need not be a discouraging exercise. Rather, it should be exhilarating to see that we are improving day by day.

- *Measuring progress*: It is helpful to document our current state and highlight milestones, so that we can visualize our progress. Witnessing our own growth and development is, by itself, a powerful motivator.

- *Keeping our ego at bay*: If we do not approach this as a learning activity, we can either become discouraged by our failures or arrogant when reviewing our successes. To avoid this pitfall, it is critical to keep the ego out of the way. To do so we view the process not as a verdict of good or bad, but as a tool to track our learning.

3) *Form an image of how we would look and feel, and what we would experience if we were practicing the capability:* Visualizing a desired outcome is a powerful way to move towards that goal. We can draw on inspiring examples to know how particular qualities, skills or capabilities look when manifested in a person's life. We can then use such examples as templates for growth. We can also practice *living from the future*, imagining ourselves practicing the capability and experiencing the feelings we would have as we do so.

4) *Set specific goals, identify intermediate steps and take action to accomplish them:* It is often helpful to break down a quality or skill that we wish to acquire into smaller steps, so that we are not overwhelmed by the enormity of the task. For example, if we wish to be in better control of outbursts of anger and remain calm in difficult situations, we might take a particular situation in which we displayed anger and follow the sequence of steps that led to our losing control. Just as a mental model may result in automatic pre-determined responses, so too, certain sequences of events may lead us to outbursts of anger. We can deconstruct the anger "mental model" by using the same methodology we did in Chapters II and III by: gaining insight into our thoughts and behaviors, analyzing the effects of our behaviors on others, and understanding the subsequent impact on our relationships. Then, as we learn to identify the triggers, we can contain the feeling of anger and consciously decide how to *respond*, rather than *react* without thinking.

▶ ESSENTIAL QUALITIES AND ATTITUDE

Self-evaluation and the subsequent efforts leading to transformation require *determination, humility*, and *constancy*. When the spirit of service, rather than an egotistic desire to excel, motivates this effort, it will contribute to the development of transformative leadership.

When undertaken with an underlying *posture of learning*, self-evaluation becomes a tool for growth and development. Without it, self-evaluation may degenerate into destructive self-criticism, or if carried out too superficially, becomes ineffective. Therefore, to effectively develop the capability of self-evaluation, we recognize that we are embarked on a life-long journey of learning, in which difficulties, setbacks, and challenges are to be expected – even necessary – for us to realize our full potential.

LEARNING FROM REFLECTION ON ACTION

Learning is a product of dynamic interaction with knowledge. The knowledge can be gleaned either from experience or from experts, books, or other sources that we consider reliable. However, learning only takes place if we interact with that knowledge. The two primary means of interaction are *reflection* and *action*. These four aspects of learning — *experience, conceptualization, reflection* and *action* — can be diagrammed in the form of a learning cycle.

All of life is an *experience*. Spontaneous *reflection* on real life experiences is the first step in generating a *concept*. Through repeated reflection, we can expand, elaborate, and refine our concepts. However, if we are to benefit from a concept, we need to work with it and apply it. This step requires *action,* putting into practice the conclusions reached in the conceptualization. The process is iterative, since the *ac-*

tion taken creates new *experiences*, which can lead to further *reflection*

and to a more complete and better-understood *conceptualization*. The learning cycle can also begin by acquiring a new *concept*. After attempting to apply the concept through *action*, we *reflect* on the resulting *experience* and 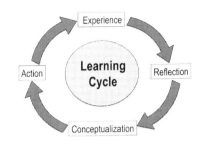 then revise and improve our understanding of the *concept*.

Without adequate *reflection*, our ability to learn is impaired. When things go badly, we frequently hear the comment, "Chalk that one up to experience," implying that at least the experience was useful in teaching us what not to do. However, we usually do not learn from experience, because we don't take time to reflect on what happened, why it happened and what we could have done differently. As a consequence, the next time we often react as we did the time before and have a similar experience. Without *reflection*, we learn little or nothing from experience. However, when we reflect on our experiences, seeking to understand the lessons they bring us, they become means to a deeper understanding of life. Therefore, reflection is an essential aspect of *transformative learning*. Without it, we may acquire information, but that information does not result in new ways of thinking and acting.

When we do engage in reflection, it is often spontaneous and incomplete. Therefore, our learning process will be faster and more productive if we are systematic and guide our *reflection* by a list of questions, such as: "What did I expect to happen? What really happened? Why did it happen? What were the positive and negative aspects of the situation? What can I learn from this? What would I do differently if I had the chance to relive the situation?"

Groups and organizations can also benefit from systematically reflecting on their experiences. Without the conscious recognition of the learning opportunities brought by experience, we risk repeating automatic reactions even when these don't bring the desired results, simply because we have developed mental models that automatically evoke pre-programmed reactions.

It is also possible to read or study without reflecting, merely adding the contents to the knowledge already stored in memory. Peter Senge and colleagues call this kind of learning *reactive learning*,[1] since it tends to be superficial and doesn't really change behavior. We prefer Mezirow's terminology, *informative learning*,[2] because we may indeed become better informed about a certain topic. However, it is not until we challenge the underlying assumptions of our mental models and deeply reflect on our actions from a learning posture that we can expect our behaviors to change.

By choosing to be proactive in our learning and purposefully *reflecting* on our actions in order to understand what works and what doesn't, what is effective and what isn't, what is based on truth and what is flawed, we are engaging in reflective learning, which is *transformative* rather than *informative*. We can visualize this process as one of 'emptying' ourselves of preconceived ideas and *letting go* of our points of view in order for the truth to emerge. As we become more aware of this truth and *let it come* into our consciousness, a new con-

Informative (Reactive) Learning
(adapted from Peter Senge, et. al.)

Thinking
"Downloading"
Mental Models

Action
Re-enacting
Habitual Patterns

ceptual framework takes root, allowing acquisition of new learning and new capabilities.

MIT's innovation theorist, Otto Scharmer, explains in his book, *Theory U*, that many failed attempts to address the prevailing challenges of our times result from fundamental blindness to the deeper dimensions of effective change. Accessing those deeper dimensions or illuminating the "blind spots" can be facilitated through a process he calls *presencing*, or "learning from the emerging future." This process is shaped like a 'U' and summarizes the kind of learning that results in transformation.[3]

Transformative (Reflective) Learning
(Overview of learning process; adapted from O. Scharmer)

Awareness of Mental Models

Fuller Understanding of Reality

Letting Go

New Behaviors

New Capabilities

New Learning

New Conceptual Framework

Letting Come

The process is one in which the downward slope represents deep reflection and detachment from our limited understanding, while the upward slope represents new understanding based on truth and its manifestations in action.

Each new insight will challenge our unexamined assumptions and inspire us to modify our actions, thereby generating new experiences. These will then lead to further reflection and learning. This iterative process provides increasingly deeper understanding of the truth of a situation and how we might achieve our objectives. This kind of learning, because it changes how we think, has a profound effect on our actions. We cease to react mindlessly because the structure of our thinking has changed profoundly. The reflection process has negated faulty assumptions and disrupted our mental models. As a result, our automatic reactions are replaced by thoughtful responses, based on new understanding, born from new insights. Transformative learning, then, involves the transformation of unconscious mental models into conscious, thoughtfully elaborated *conceptual frameworks*.

▶ TOOLS FOR EXPLORING MENTAL MODELS

Since mental models contain only part, but not all of the truth, they limit learning. To overcome this limitation, we use tools that help us appreciate that our beliefs about the world and different aspects of life are not absolute truths, but rather a product of our unique cultural background and life experiences. This recognition creates within us the receptivity to explore, accept and integrate new knowledge. One such tool is the *ladder of inference*, first described by organizational psychologist, Chris Argyris and further elaborated by Peter Senge.[4] It reveals how we routinely, though unconsciously, slant our experiences to reinforce pre-existing biases. Throughout our lives we are exposed to a wide variety of information from the world around us. However, we do not take in all information. We *select* the information we use. This selection is based on our culture, history and life experiences that inform us about what is relevant and acceptable and what is not.

We attach meaning to our choices and *interpret* what the information means based on our past experiences and cultural context. We make *assumptions* based on the meanings that we attach to the information we have selected. We draw *conclusions* about those assumptions. From that, we adopt *beliefs* about the world and how it works. We then take *actions* based on those be-

Ladder of Inference
(adapted from Peter Senge)

- Taking Action
- Forming Beliefs
- Drawing Conclusions
- Making Assumptions
- Interpreting Meaning
- Selecting Data
- Observing Facts

liefs. Those beliefs and actions become the basis upon which we select and interpret future data, which then further reinforces our assumptions, our conclusions, our beliefs and actions. These continually feed back to strengthen the mental model this process has previously created and repeatedly reinforced.

Understanding these important unconscious steps in our processing of information is essential for critical scrutiny of mental models, for we can then see where — *on which level of the ladder of inference* — we might have erred in our evaluation of data. When others do not see things the way we do, we can actually take them up our ladder of inference so that they will understand how we arrived at our beliefs and actions. They can do the same for us and permit us to view their thought processes. Understanding this internal system permits us to ask, "Upon what data do you base your beliefs and actions?" Then we can consider adjustments if we selected the wrong information to focus on or if we attached incorrect meaning and arrived at faulty assumptions.

In the exploration of any topic, we need to ask ourselves:

1) What does the evidence show?

2) Am I looking at all the evidence or am I selecting according to my biases?

3) What does it mean?

4) What are the assumptions I am making and what am I basing them on?

5) Are my conclusions consistent with objective evidence?

6) Are my beliefs and actions consistent with objective evidence and ethical principles?

If we simply add information without doing this kind of reality check, our new knowledge will have a shaky foundation. However, once we have a systematic mechanism for checking the logic and consistency of our thinking, we can have confidence that our education will be empowering. Now we are on the path to transformative learning.

This process of scrutiny may seem straightforward, but rarely are we even aware that we are operating based on unexamined assumptions. However, when there are inconsistencies and contradictions in our thinking, they can usually be traced to conflicting mental models related to different aspects of life. For example, we may have one mental model that describes how the economy operates, another related to scientific knowledge, and still another related to religion. Our mental model of the economy may contain ideas related to individualism, free enterprise, and freedom from regulation. Our mental model of science will very likely include the concept of evolution. Our mental model of religion probably includes the concept that God created man and the hope for a better world free from poverty.

Are there any inconsistencies among the above mental models? Is a belief in evolution compatible with the belief that God created man? Are the ideas related to the economy compatible with the elimination of poverty and the creation of a more just world? What are the unexamined assumptions? How must the ideas in each model be understood, modified or practiced in order for them to be truly coherent one with another? These are the types of questions each of us must ask and answer for ourselves when we begin to examine the mental models we use to organize our understanding of truth and determine how best to behave. Unless we compare our mental models to one another, reflect on the implications of differing assumptions, and attempt to reconcile them, these contradictions will lead to inconsistencies in our thoughts and actions. By facing and resolving such apparent or real contradictions, we achieve coherence in our thoughts and authenticity in our actions.

Since we are not consciously aware of our mental models, any step toward changing them requires that we become aware of and disturbed by their incompatible contents. Often a crisis in our life forces us to re-examine our thinking. However, we do not have to wait for a crisis in order to engage in this process. We can choose to be proactive and make use of any of the following approaches to aid us in the process of questioning our mental models.

1) Employ the *ladder of inference*, in order to understand how we have arrived at our beliefs.

2) Analyze the degree to which our mental model corresponds to reality by identifying *internal inconsistencies*, exposing logical fallacies, or contrasting the mental model with scientific evidence and ethical principles, as we did with the mental models related to human nature and society in Chapter II.

3) Identify the *effects* of the mental model, as we did with the prevailing mental models of leadership in Chapter III.

4) Contrast a new *conceptual framework* with the mental model and evaluate its comparative strengths.

Critical analysis is the first step in liberating us from the power of a flawed mental model. However, we need something with which to replace it. A consciously elaborated *conceptual framework* coherent with universal ethical values and scientific evidence can greatly facilitate the transformation of mental models into new ways of thinking and acting that are based in truth and conducive to transformation.

A conceptual framework is similar to a mental model in the sense that it is a way of thinking that influences our actions. However, it has several characteristics that distinguish it from a mental model. It is *conscious, logical, evolving and coherent with evidence and ethical princi-*

ples. When we know what we think about something and why, we are able to formulate it in a clear and concise way. We are able to reflect on it in order to eliminate any inconsistencies. We are open to, even eager for, new information to deepen our understanding and welcome challenges to our thinking. When we discover new aspects of truth, we willingly broaden, modify or even make major changes in our conceptual

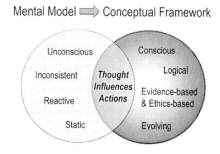

framework. We are no longer attached to tradition or the comfort of unexamined ways of thinking; we are attached to truth.

▶ From Transformative Learning to Transformed Behavior

In transformative learning, a fundamental shift occurs in our frame of reference, leading to the adoption of a new conceptual framework. However, aligning action with this new, enlightened understanding is also a learning process. While the insight into new ways of perceiving and understanding reality may occur instantly, aligning action with those insights is usually a lifelong journey.

The process of creating a just, united, peaceful society — or even an institution with these characteristics — is a very ambitious and transformative initiative. The path to achieving it is uncharted and untested. Although we know that there are certain universal principles that should guide our actions, we are the ones who need to blaze the trail. Even though this may appear intimidating, it is less overwhelming once we recognize that it is *a learning process* requiring small steps in the right direction that, over time, will bring us closer to our goal.

Due to the critical role of learning in the transformation process, we begin by embracing a learning posture, proactively seeking out learning opportunities and cultivating attitudes conducive to learning. We are willing to question our own ideas, modify our beliefs, relentlessly search for truth, and courageously embrace the truths we discover, even at the cost of our own self-interest.

SYSTEMIC THINKING

When we engage in *systemic thinking*, we see the object of study as part of a greater system. We take into account the relationships among the parts of the system, between the parts and the whole, and between the whole and larger systems in which it is embedded. We recognize and accept complexity and interdependence. We do not accept simplistic solutions simply for the sake of momentarily resolving pressing problems. Rather, we consider the long-term *impact* that a proposed solution will have on the whole system and recognize that any so-called solution that merely passes the problem on to another part of the system is not truly a solution. For example, solving the problem of radioactive wastes by selling them to other countries simply shifts the problem from one part of the global community to another. It doesn't solve the problem.

Systemic thinking can be contrasted with *linear thought*. Linear thought seeks only one cause for each phenomenon rather than a multitude of interacting factors. It fragments knowledge into discrete disciplines rather than integrating knowledge across disciplines. It isolates pieces of the system rather than looking for the order implicit in the entire system. It proposes partial, simplistic solutions to problems that ultimately affect the entire system, rather than getting at the root of the problem by addressing issues in a systemic way. A good example of systemic thinking is found in the science of ecology, which is concerned with the relationships among organisms and their complex environments.

Our tendency to engage in systemic thinking versus linear thought may depend on our mental models. If we grew up among people who practice systemic thinking, it may seem natural to us. But if those around us have always used linear thought, we may initially resist the need for systemic thinking, because we selectively focus on information that concurs with our mental models. Furthermore, we will be able to find myriads of examples to support our predisposition to linear thought. However, if we make the effort to think systemically, we will begin to perceive networks of relationships that mutually influence one another. Consequently our understanding will improve in both breadth and depth.

The Drowning Children

A man was standing on the bank of a river, when suddenly he saw a child who was about to drown. Forgetful of his own safety, he threw himself into the river, and with great effort was able to save the child.

He was scarcely recovering when, much to his surprise, he saw another child drowning. In spite of his extreme tiredness, he once again threw himself into the river, and was able to save the second child.

He felt completely exhausted when he saw the third child come bobbing down the river. He doubted that he had the strength to also save that one, but he decided to make the effort. Using his last ounce of strength, he saved the third child.

But he also began to ask himself: "How can it be that one after another three children were drowning in the river? There seems to be a repetitive pattern that must have an explanation."

He looked upriver and saw a man throwing children into the river every five minutes. He finally understood what he had to do.

▶ Systems Archetypes

When we engage in systemic thinking, we are aware that events can be interpreted at three levels. First, we perceive *isolated events*. Second, we become aware that the event is part of a recurrent *pattern*. Seeing the event as part of a pattern motivates us to try to see it in a larger context and to identify some of the interactions and interrelationships between the particular event and other related instances. We may have to observe the event and its surrounding context during an extended period of time before we become aware of these relationships. During this process we need an open mind, a tolerance for ambiguity, and patience. This will gradually lead us to the third, and deepest level of analysis, in which we attempt to identify the *systemic structure* that induces the pattern.

Systems experts have discovered that there are certain structures called *systems archetypes* that recur over and over in many different fields. "Systems archetypes," explains Peter Senge, "are analogous to …simple stories that get retold again and again."[5] Once we identify the systemic structure that is inducing a particular pattern, it is easier to see the points of leverage in the system where small changes can lead to significant differences. We can then devise and carry out systemic interventions that lead to lasting results. Although interventions at this level may be difficult to formulate and implement, and may only yield results in the long term, they are the most likely to produce enduring results because the solution is based on an understanding of the system and on the effects that different types of interventions may have. While it is most effective to address a problem at the systemic level, it may also be necessary to complement that approach with immediate, temporary interventions that mitigate negative symptoms.

For example, if a student fails a history test, his parents may first respond to it as an *isolated event.* They may simply accept his explanation that the teacher gave a surprise test with difficult questions because she was upset with the class. Or they may react, scolding him and exhorting him to study more. But as long as they perceive the situation as an isolated event, they are not likely to initiate an ongoing plan of action. However, if in the course of the following months their son also fails tests in other subjects, they will probably become aware that failing tests is becoming a *recurrent pattern*. Once they perceive the pattern, they will be more likely to take action to solve the problem. They may begin studying with their son before every test to make sure that he is well prepared. This solution may be successful as long as the parents dedicate time and energy to finding out when their son will have tests, and then studying with him. But as soon as something prevents them from studying with him, he may immediately fail again. This may happen repeatedly because they have been treating the symptom (failing tests) rather than the problem (what is causing him to fail). This type of response is so common, it is known as *shifting the burden.* [6]

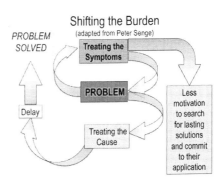

Shifting the Burden
(adapted from Peter Senge)

▶▶ SHIFTING THE BURDEN

In the systems archetype of *shifting the burden*, actions to alleviate the symptoms of a problem diminish the perceived need to take actions to treat its cause. As a result, the problem continues recurring periodically and the symptomatic solution must be continually invoked.

Once the parents become aware that they are shifting the burden, they may ask themselves, "What is the cause of the problem? Why does our son tend to fail tests in these particular subjects?" This may lead them to awareness that all the subjects that their son fails demand a high degree of reading comprehension. They may then discover that their son has not developed the skills to identify the main idea of what he reads, to see the relationship between the main idea and supporting details, to make summaries, and to ask himself questions about what he reads as he reads it. They may also realize that they do not spend much time with their son except when they are helping him study, and that failing tests may be a way of getting parental time and attention. Helping their son to develop reading comprehension skills and restructuring personal lifestyles to spend more shared time with their son in activities that he enjoys will probably be harder and more time-consuming than simply helping him to prepare for each test. But the solution will be definitive because it gets at the *root of the problem*. While applying this long-term solution, the parents will probably want to continue helping their son prepare for his tests (an immediate, temporary intervention), then, gradually give him ever-greater responsibility to do so on his own.

▶▶ Limits to Growth

Another systems archetype is known as *limits to growth*.[7] In this case, a successful process with continuous growth begins to encounter opposition that makes further growth much more difficult. When we become aware of this pattern, we need to identify both the direct forces that lead to the desired end as well as the forces that are obstructing it. Then we take action to lessen the opposing forces. Peter Senge explains that reducing the opposing forces leads to more permanent solutions than taking action to increase the direct forces, because the latter has the undesirable effect of generating even greater opposition.

For example, when rural schoolteachers in Latin America, who had been trained as community development agents, began to teach transformative leadership, in some communities the traditional leaders felt threatend and began to take actions to undermine the program. The most effective response was for the teachers to explain the program to the leaders, assuring them that they had no intention of usurping their position, and offering to involve them in the program in a prestigious way. This allayed the concerns of the leaders and most of the negative comments and actions ceased. If, however, the teachers had simply stepped up their own activities with the community, without seeking to neutralize the opposition of the leaders, the conflict would have increased.

▶ Requirements

1) *Self-discipline*: Systemic thinking is a capability that must be patiently cultivated and requires self-discipline. Instead of impulsively adopting a solution, we need to take time to look for and thoroughly analyze different factors and their interrelations before initiating action.

2) *Commitment to truth*: We need the ability to see a problem or event from various perspectives to understand its entirety. Searching out a diversity of viewpoints and using a trans-disciplinary approach to problem-solving facilitates this process.

3) *Consultation*: The ability to consult in groups with an open mind helps us to find the truth embodied in each perspective, to understand the relationship between the various aspects of truth, and to see how truths discovered through the group consultation process shed light on the problem and its solution.

▶ Order Out of Chaos

There is another aspect of systemic thinking that has to do with making sense out of chaos. If we can identify the variables in a situation, patterns will emerge. Patterns are easy to detect if there are only a few variables operating, as in the example of the person throwing children into the river. Sometimes there are more variables leading to more complex relationships which careful analysis, often aided by group consultation, brings to light. This can be seen in the examples given regarding the systems archetypes of *shifting the burden* and *limits to growth*. It takes more investigation and analysis to see the patterns of *systemic structures*.

However, there are times that the variables are so numerous that they cannot all be identified; some may not even be known. In fact, in such non-linear systems, the outcomes may be so unpredictable that the system is thought to be *random* or *chaotic*. In such a system, under the right conditions, a very small change can lead to unpredictably large, even catastrophic outcomes. This phenomenon is known as the *"butterfly effect."* The meteorologist, Edward Lorenz, coined this term in 1960, when he was studying weather patterns using a computer model. In such non-linear systems, he concluded, under the right conditions, a small change, such as *"the flap of a butterfly's wings,"* can result in a hurricane thousands of miles away. This was the origin of chaos theory.[8]

Over the next few decades, the field grew rapidly with applications not only in mathematics and multiple areas of science, but also in the social sciences, economics and philosophy. In fact, implications can be drawn for any system considered to be non-linear with sensitive initial conditions. One of the more exciting developments in the field stems from the work of Ilya Prigogine who won the Nobel Prize in physical chemistry in 1977. He was able to show that a system that is far from equilibrium gives rise to "dissipative structures," a prelude to self-organization at a higher level of order. Or, stated another way, when a system has reached a certain pitch of chaotic activity, it can become transformed and attain a *higher level of order*. In his book, *Order Out of Chaos,*[9] he explains how this works in chemistry. However, subsequently, he drew implications, as did others, for the social sciences as well. As Fritjof Capra explains, "This spontaneous emergence of order at critical points of instability is now one of the most important concepts of the new understanding of life. It is technically known as self-organization and is often referred to simply as 'emergence.' It has been recognized as the dynamic origin of development, learning and evolution." [10]

If we reflect on the current crises encompassing the world, and the seemingly random, even chaotic events, it would not be hard to conclude that we may be approaching a turning point. Could it prove to be a prelude to collective transformation and a higher level of order?

CREATIVE INITIATIVE

Taking initiative implies doing something on our own without needing to be asked or reminded. Behind initiative lies the conscious intention and desire to do something, even when we may not have a clear idea at first of exactly what we will do or how we will do it.

There are different types of initiatives. *Routine initiatives* are related to familiar actions or activities. They can range from something as simple as washing the dishes to more complex activities, such as training doctors to do surgery. What makes the initiative routine is that it is a commonly realized activity with known and accepted procedures. Initiative is necessary because the motivation to arise and carry out the activity comes from within. Routine initiatives are needed, praiseworthy, and usually receive little resistance from others.

Creative initiatives bring into being something new that did not exist before. Works of music, dance, and the arts fall in this category. They enrich human life and create beauty. In fact, all acts that are expressions of the aesthetic urge to create beauty spring from creative initiative. There is another type of creative initiative, however, undertaken to effect significant change. This kind of creative initiative often generates resistance from those who see no need to do things differently and requires courage and perseverance to carry to completion. Such initiatives are necessary in order to reorient focus, prevent stagnation and promote progress.

All forms of initiative imply freely chosen activities. Therefore, they are expressions of *human volition*, or *will*. Since volition is internal, the initial phases of initiative are invisible to all except the person taking the initiative. By acquiring knowledge of the *seven phases of initiative*, we can analyze where we are in the process, see with greater clarity the next step we need to take, and consequently carry more of our initiatives to completion. These phases are:

1) *Intention*
2) *Purpose*
3) *Concrete planning*
4) *Commitment*
5) *Permission*
6) *Opportune timing*
7) *Realization in the physical world*

Initiative begins with our sincere *intention* to do something in a certain field of action. Once we focus our intention by defining a specific *purpose,* the initiative takes on form and direction. Next, *concrete planning* is necessary in order to define the actions and resources we need. These first three phases lead to clarity of thought and strengthen our resolve. In the next phase we make a firm *commitment* to implement the vision when the opportunity arises. Commitment is comprised of three elements: *determination* to carry out the plan, *confidence* that we will obtain everything necessary to do so, and assured, vigorous and timely *action*. Next we need *permission* to carry out the initiative. It might be official permission required by some institution or organization, permission granted by circumstances that facilitate the needed actions, or internal permission, which means simply feeling assurance about going ahead. If external permission is needed and takes time to obtain, instead of becoming impatient, we can accept the delay as part of the process, while taking every possible action to facilitate the granting of permission. For every initiative there is an *appropriate time* and a suitable duration. These are often determined by circumstances in the world around us. We need to be aware of appropriate opportunities to implement our initiative. When the time is right, we carry out the planned activities so that the initiative comes into existence in the contingent world. When the initiative is completed, what had formerly only existed in the world of thought is *realized in the physical world.*

Learning to *consciously work through these phases* enhances our capability of taking creative, disciplined initiative. When we know what phase we are in and what the following phase should be, we can see the next step more clearly and take appropriate action to implement it. This allows us to consciously progress through the different phases until the initiative becomes a reality. At times we may traverse these phases rapidly; but when we get stuck or encounter obstacles, insight into the process becomes critical in our persevering and not giving up prematurely.

When we are engaged in realizing a creative initiative, we also need to recognize that there is another very subtle independent process operating: the process of collective social advancement. As human social organization evolves, new institutions, discoveries, arts, and systems come into being to serve the newfound capacities. As these emerge, individuals serve as *instruments* of beauty and progress. We help what is emerging to become reality — through what is often referred to as *inspiration*. Knowledge of the phases of initiative can help us to become more effective instruments of progress. We can engage in the transformative process by releasing our own preconceived ideas (*letting go*) so that we can be fully present, allow inspiration to act through us and serve as effective conduits for what is emerging (*letting come*). Being aware that we serve as *instruments* for something much greater than ourselves can give us the necessary courage and motivation to persevere through the various phases of initiative.

PERSEVERANCE

Although initiating a project is an important achievement, carrying it through to conclusion demands effort and perseverance. The capability of *persevering* in the achievement of a goal is related to the degree to which we identify with the vision that has inspired that goal. When a project is inspired by a vision and by transcendent values similar to those we cherish, our commitment to the project is much greater than if we are not conscious of such a relationship. The alignment between the project's goals and our personal vision gives us a sense of ownership and inspires us to make whatever effort and sacrifice the project demands.

▶ PLANNING

Once commitment exists, we need to plan the project in such a way that work is phased and systematic. Careful planning facilitates perseverance by assuring that the work can be sustained over time, so that we do not exhaust ourselves in the early stages of the project, and then feel like giving up halfway through. A well-planned project will:

1) clearly articulate the desired results,

2) include indicators that will demonstrate when success has been achieved,

3) program activities that will meet targeted milestones,

4) anticipate and strategize for obstacles that may arise,

5) calculate and obtain needed resources, and

6) appropriately pace the work.

The level of detail that should be included in the planning depends on the type of project. Elaborate planning is particularly useful when both the outcome and the steps to achieve it are well understood, such as the construction of a building. However, elaborate planning can be counterproductive in a creative initiative aiming to bring about innovation. The less predictable and controllable the factors in an initiative, the more flexible the planning should be.

▶ ANTICIPATING PROBLEMS

It is normal for problems and obstacles to arise in every project. By accepting this fact, and even welcoming the problems as learning opportunities, we can avoid becoming impatient or frustrated when they do. Successfully meeting such challenges requires that we engage in an iterative process of action and reflection. Each iteration of the cycle results in new learning and increasingly effective action. At times when chaos reigns, we may find ourselves walking in a fog where only a few points of reference are clear. We must learn to be comfortable with such ambiguity as we struggle to find effective solutions to vexing obstacles.

Problems, far from causing discouragement, must be seen as opportunities for learning — tests naturally encountered to hone our capacities and bring out our best. When we feel overwhelmed by a problem, we must be able to transcend the immediate situation, see the problem from a broader perspective and draw upon sources of strength that enable us to renew and reinvigorate our efforts.

On a practical level, we need to view problems systemically. We can gain insight into challenges by examining the interrelationships among the various elements that give rise to the problem and look for patterns. This will help us to distinguish symptoms from causes and avoid superficial actions that only alleviate the symptoms when what are needed are more far-reaching, difficult changes in structures or values. Furthermore, we can analyze the forces that are impeding results and take specific actions to diminish those forces.

To summarize, any project, no matter how well-conceived or creatively initiated, will fail to reach a successful conclusion without tenacious perseverance and constant effort to overcome obstacles. Perseverance requires *determination* that is detached from preconceived solutions and is open to unexpected possibilities that arise in the problem-solving process. Since this attitude of openness implies living with uncertainty and the stress of unresolved problems, perseverance requires *self-discipline*. Above all, especially when striving for complex change, perseverance is about learning. Having a learning attitude makes all the difference between giving up prematurely and persevering through the long haul to victory.

SELF-DISCIPLINE

Any achievement in life requires self-discipline, whether in sports, education, professional work, or transformative leadership. If we wish to improve our performance or become outstanding in our area of endeavor, we must discipline ourselves to overcome those things that might adversely affect our mastery. Our free will allows us to direct our thoughts and actions toward specific goals. We can turn toward nobility and develop lofty purposes and capabilities or we can allow ourselves to succumb to base passions and selfish desires, never achieving our true purpose.

While the satisfaction of physical appetites gives a certain kind of pleasure, this pleasure is limited and fleeting. Those who seek physical pleasure to excess often find that pleasure turning bitter or tedious. Worse yet, the need for a particular kind of physical sensation may gradually become insatiable, requiring ever more frequent and greater doses of the stimulant in order to achieve ever more momentary satisfaction. This is obviously true for addictive substances such as drugs and alcohol, but may also be true for other physical pleasures carried to excess, like overeating.

Conversely, we experience deep satisfaction and self-mastery when we exercise *self-discipline* by avoiding short-term pleasures that may harm others or us and consciously make choices that have long-term, positive effects on our lives. Actions that help us improve our capabilities and bring about meaningful achievements contribute to self-actualization. We never become satiated by these sources of fulfillment, as they create opportunities for endless growth and development. We are motivated to practice self-discipline when we recognize that our long-term happiness depends on it. Consequently, we are more willing to make a daily effort to direct our passions towards higher purposes and

154

to acquire the knowledge, skills, attitudes, and qualities that lead to the development of those capabilities.

There are multiple levels that require the practice of self-discipline. Stephen Covey outlines three distinct levels:

1) control and guide the appropriate expression of our physical appetites and develop discipline related to other aspects of our material well-being;

2) quell our tendencies towards pride and the desire to impress others; and

3) resist the ambition for power over others.

Self-discipline must be cultivated through daily practice. Covey advises us to *sharpen the saw* daily: physically, by keeping our bodies in shape; intellectually, by continual learning; emotionally, by cultivating patience, empathy, and personal responsibility; and spiritually, by praying and meditating.[11]

The key to developing self-discipline is dedication to a vision that reflects our highest values. Then, we exercise *willpower* and *consistent effort* to keep our eyes and actions focused on that vision. Finally, we consciously *cultivate humility* and *a spirit of service* so that, rather than feeling proud about our progress and achievements, we remain focused on our goal of contributing to the common good.

RECTITUDE OF CONDUCT

Rectitude of conduct can be defined as behavior that accepts appropriate responsibility, is guided by ethical principles, aligns deeds with words and assumes responsibility for consequences. One characteristic that distinguishes a mature adult from a child is precisely the ability to consciously make and carry out decisions based on principles, while being accountable for the results. For example, when confronted with a problem, we choose to accept or reject responsibility for solving it, rather than reacting automatically. If we recognize that we *own* the problem, we are responsible for contributing to its solution, rather than simply blaming others. If we decide the problem is not ours and we do not accept the responsibility, we need to detach ourselves from the results, allowing those who are responsible to manage the situation as they see best, without blaming them for what they do.

At times we erroneously accept responsibility for tasks or problems that belong to others. This is particularly true if we tend to be paternalistic. For example, if two colleagues are upset with one another, we may try to help them to reconcile their differences and feel frustrated if we are not successful. However, in this case the responsibility to resolve the problem is theirs, not ours. Although we may offer them suggestions or encouragement, we cannot force them to reconcile. However, if their problem affects our work, we need to take responsibility for resolving this aspect of the problem.

More often, however, rather than accepting too much responsibility, we refuse to accept our share of responsibility for problems. We tend to blame others, wait passively for the problem to resolve itself, or demand that others resolve it. For example, when a child has difficulties at school, the teacher often blames the parents, the parents blame the teacher, and both blame the child, hoping that punishment will change his behavior. However, blaming someone only creates defensiveness and estrangement; it doesn't lead to change. Rarely do parents, teacher and child *consult*, trying to understand the root causes of the problem and determine what positive actions each could take to bring about its resolution.

In brief, when a problem occurs, it is important to 1) see the situation as clearly and objectively as possible; 2) decide who shares in the *ownership* of the problem; and 3) accept responsibility for solving our share of the problem. After accepting responsibility, the next step is to *assume* responsibility by deciding what specific actions to take, carrying out those decisions, and accepting the consequences. If some of the necessary actions require capabilities we don't have, we need to either develop those capabilities or request assistance from others.

Turning to ethical principles for guidance helps us to make wise decisions about what actions to take and what attitudes to adopt in our relationships with others. Like a compass, principles indicate the general direction to go, yet do not stifle creativity by dictating the exact path to follow. Without reference to principles, our choices are often based on our own changing whims and appetites, or on mere opinions, lacking coherence and wisdom. However, when our decisions are grounded in principles that derive from a sincere search for truth, there is coherence between our beliefs and actions that translates into a capability for rectitude of conduct and trustworthiness.

The principles upon which we base our actions must not be chosen at random, but rather, be the result of our search for truth. In this investigation, we can try to identify those principles that have been repeatedly emphasized by the great spiritual leaders in different cultures, civilizations and historic periods. This search invariably leads us to the recognition that certain principles related to love and justice have been stressed over and over again to such an extent that we could take these as *spiritual laws* — laws intrinsic to the human condition and to the positive interpersonal relationships upon which effective, prosperous organizations, institutions, and societies are built.

Rectitude of conduct also demands that our deeds match our

words. No matter how passionately we voice our noble goals and ethical principles, it is not until we demonstrate them in our actions that we can be effective agents of transformation. Of course, none of us can perfectly exemplify the high ideals that inspire us. We are all fallible and our deeds will always fall short of our words. However, continually striving to align the two is what leads to progress – the greater the alignment, the greater our rectitude of conduct.

Even though we strive to guide our actions by principles, we still have no guarantee that we will always make the best decision, or that our actions will not generate new problems of one sort or another. Thus, we also have to accept responsibility for the consequences of our actions. If some of the consequences are negative, we must have the humility to admit our mistakes and maintain a learning attitude in order to take appropriate new actions.

Striving for a high standard of rectitude of conduct with courage and uncompromising determination is, by itself, an inspiring example of transformative leadership that has the power to change us and improve our social environments.

CHAPTER VI

CAPABILITIES FOR

TRANSFORMATION OF

INTERPERSONAL RELATIONSHIPS

IMBUING THOUGHTS AND ACTIONS WITH LOVE

Human beings cannot live without love; our very survival depends on it. We need love in order to grow, to develop our potential and to give the best of ourselves. However, we often think of love primarily in terms of romantic love, or even in a wider context, as simply an emotion over which we have no control, that we either feel or do not feel towards a particular person. Love is seen as something that simply happens, rather than as a quality that we can actively develop. Consequently, we may not pause to reflect on its characteristics.

Psychologist and philosopher, Erich Fromm, redefines love as, "the active concern for the life and the growth of that which we love," characterized by care, responsibility, respect, and knowledge.[1] We can choose to actively concern ourselves with the well-being of others, to strive to know them as they really are, to communicate our understanding, to carry out actions that convey care and respect, and to act responsibly in our relationships. Consequently, this definition implies that we can consciously choose to increase our ability to love. We can actively express love towards another person, whether or not we may initially have any positive feelings. As a result of this action, however, our love begins to grow.

This definition also makes it clear that loving does not mean giving people everything they want, continually doing things for them that they should do for themselves, or simply going along with whatever they decide to do. Rather, if our loved ones want to do something that is detrimental to their well-being, that is lacking in respect for themselves or others, or that goes against universal moral principles, then true love requires that we communicate how we feel. However, despite the occasional need to oppose the desires of someone we love, (what some call "tough love") most of us need to work primarily on communicating more effectively our positive feelings of affection and appreciation for others.

Acts of love begin with loving thoughts. We can consciously direct our thoughts towards love, then look for opportunities to translate those loving thoughts into loving acts. We can choose to reach out to the many people who cross our paths each day — family members, classmates, colleagues, co-workers, and even strangers. This can begin with small actions: smiling at them, greeting them with a cheerful demeanor and friendly voice, speaking kindly without complaining or criticizing, listening with interest when they speak, sharing knowledge they might find useful, including them in activities, offering to help with their work, and spending time with them doing what they enjoy. Most importantly, it means accepting and appreciating others just the way they are, expressing joy in exploring their differences from us.

If we sincerely want to improve a problematic relationship, we can begin by strengthening our love for the person involved. We can give expression to that love by making time for meaningful interaction, listening with empathy, and focusing on his good qualities, rather than dwelling on negative traits. Not being judgmental of others while focusing on our own need to improve are essential ingredients of love.

The most highly developed expression of love is found in truly selfless love, a love where we put the well-being of the loved one before our own comfort. When it attains this level of purity, the power of love overcomes self-interest and barriers disappear. Suddenly our own needs become secondary. The most common demonstration of this can be seen in the sacrifices parents make for their children. We also see this kind of love in heroic acts and in the lives of some of the greatest leaders.

There is something almost magical about sincere love that is free from self-interest. It has the power to attract hearts — a magnetic quality that touches even the most hardened heart. So, imbuing our actions with love gives those actions a special attractive quality. It creates in others the desire to respond positively and to cooperate. It gives them greater confidence in themselves and helps them to develop their capabilities. It also amplifies our own capacity for giving love. Just as a muscle becomes stronger through exercise, so does the capability of loving. We need to realize that this capability is limitless. Sharing love responsibly with one person does not diminish the amount of love we can give to another. On the contrary, the more we love, the greater becomes our capacity to love.

We can gradually expand the circle of those we love. In childhood we begin by learning to love the members of our family. As we grow, we progressively develop love and affection for friends and classmates, for our community, and for our country. In today's world, we are being called to expand this love to embrace all humanity, regarding all as brothers and sisters with genuine concern for their well-being. If we discover that we have only progressed to a certain stage in this process, we can make a conscious effort to expand the circle of those we love, directing towards them loving thoughts, followed by acts of friendship and service. The magnetic force of this expanding circle of people being attracted together has a powerful impact on the direction of our collective evolution into a united human family.

ENCOURAGEMENT

We all have the potential to do much more with our lives and to contribute more to improving the world around us. Encouragement to serve the common good contributes to the betterment of the world and helps us to realize our potential as human beings. It helps us to appreciate our own worth, have confidence in our capabilities and achievements, and aspire to higher levels of service. A powerful source of encouragement is the recognition of our essential nobility. The following counsel helps us to become conscious of both our own nobility and the nobility of others: "Look always at the good and not at the bad. If a man has ten good qualities and one bad one, look at the ten and forget the one. And if a man has ten bad qualities and one good one, look at the one and forget the ten."[2]

By focusing our attention on people's positive qualities, or even on one positive quality, we can encourage them to express their strengths, develop their potential and overcome those defects that inhibit their development. When we notice the good that others do, it motivates them to continue making similar efforts. Since people tend to respond to our expectations, sincere, positive feedback brings joy to their hearts, helps them to believe in their own potential and inspires them to develop their latent capabilities.

▶ AUTHENTIC PRAISE AND ACCEPTANCE

While we should look for positive qualities in others and appreciate them, excessive, generalized, or undeserved praise loses its positive impact and can even generate negative results, such as an inflated ego or complacency. It might also make others doubt our sincerity. We must be sincere and specific in expressing praise in order for it to be effective in encouraging others. Effective praise describes the specific, positive actions we observe in others and the positive feelings those actions have generated, while avoiding generalizations. For example, saying: "Your explanation impressed me. It was very clear and well-organized," will have a much more positive effect than a vague assertion, such as, "You are a good speaker."

Praise is not the only way to encourage and motivate others. True encouragement accepts people as they are, without judgment or pressure to change. Simply surrounding them with love while communicating confidence in them has a powerful effect. If people feel judged, they become defensive and center their actions on avoiding and/or rebutting criticism. The result is safe behaviors that inhibit growth. Conversely, when people feel accepted, they have the confidence to analyze their own mental models and behaviors and become receptive to change. In brief, we will be more effective in helping others in their development if we focus on their essential nobility, have confidence in their capacity to resolve their own problems and concentrate our commentaries on appreciating their positive actions and qualities.

▶ Inclusion

In the workplace, we can take a number of further actions to encourage and motivate others. People feel valued when we show sincere interest in their ideas and invite them to participate in consultation or in significant activities. When we recognize their potential and give them opportunities to use their capabilities, they may scale heights that even surprise themselves. When we help them see how their contributions can assist in the fulfillment of an inspiring institutional vision, they find even greater meaning and satisfaction in their work. When people feel valued, are actively engaged in developing their capabilities and find meaning in their work, they will usually attain a level of fulfillment that motivates them to strive for excellence.

▶ Abundance

In order to give encouragement, we need to have a positive, generous attitude towards life. Then our joy and enthusiasm will be contagious. We will have enough confidence in ourselves and in life that we will be able to wish for and delight in the success of others without feeling envious or fearful that their progress will hurt our own. If our worldview is one of *abundance* — an underlying belief that there is plenty for everyone — we will be more likely to encourage and support others. We will recognize the truth that the more we give, the more we ourselves receive. We will also rejoice in the knowledge that the more success we all have in serving the common good, the more rapidly the world will progress in the process of social transformation.

On the other hand, if our worldview is based on *scarcity*, we fear that the achievements of others will diminish us. We will not appreciate their success unless we have directly contributed to it and receive credit for having done so. We will have trouble congratulating them or encouraging them because we fear they may replace us, or may receive recognition that might have been ours. We also run the risk of succumbing to gossip and backbiting, twin destructive practices that are the principal causes of disunity, indifference, apathy, alienation, and withdrawal of individuals from group activities.

Some may consider that an optimistic or pessimistic attitude towards life depends on factors outside our control, such as our personality or the amount of encouragement or criticism we have experienced in our own lives. Without discounting the influence of these factors, if we maintain a deterministic attitude, we are denying our own essential nobility, and with it the responsibility we have to develop this important capability of transformative leadership.

▶ SELF-ENCOURAGEMENT

If we do not feel good about ourselves and find it difficult to encourage others, we can begin by lovingly encouraging *ourselves* first. Developing a strong commitment to an inspiring vision based on universal moral values, or drawing on our relationship to the transcendent power in the universe, can help us become more joyous and independent of the negative environmental influences that surround us. This, in turn, frees us from being overly susceptible to the judgment of others. Taking time for ourselves — engaging each week in a few activities that we enjoy — will make us feel more positive. Then we can proactively nurture the four main dimensions of our lives: physically, through good nutrition, exercise and moderation in satisfying our appetites; intellectually, by learning something new that interests us; emotionally, by engaging in fulfilling activities with friends and loved ones; and spiritually, by spending time each day in contemplative activities such as inspirational reading, meditation, or prayer. As we learn to love and care for ourselves, we will begin to experience the joy of our own unfolding growth and will become better able to love and care for others.

Paradoxically, however, the most powerful way of nurturing ourselves is by engaging in service to others. Therefore, while self-improvement is important, by itself, it is insufficient in releasing our potential to offer our best, both to ourselves and to others.

EFFECTIVE GROUP CONSULTATION

> *No power can exist except through unity. No welfare and no well-being can be attained except through consultation.*[3]
>
> *— Bahá'u'lláh*

Consultation, or more precisely, *group consultation*, is a form of discussion that fosters collective decision-making. It is a means for seeking consensus without contention and a method for making *just* decisions that take into account the well-being of all, based on the *investigation of truth* in a loving, united atmosphere. Those striving to uphold justice in decision-making must consider the well-being of all stakeholders and base decisions on the broadest possible knowledge of the relevant facts. Therefore, just decisions require the investigation of truth. Such an investigation implies exploring an issue from a *diversity* of perspectives in an environment in which those perspectives are *heard* and give rise to a more complete understanding.

▶ DIVERSITY OF VIEWS

The process of investigating truth requires a free exchange of points of view related to a topic, in which all participants are equally respected without regard for their social or professional status. As diverse ideas are dispassionately examined, taken up, left to one side, revised, integrated, or built upon, a fuller understanding gradually comes to light, reflecting the richness of a diversity of approaches.

The opinion of a very articulate person sometimes predominates in a discussion because that person may be perceived to be more intelligent. However, according to John Gardner's theory of *multiple intelligences,* which is gaining favor within education and developmental psychology, human beings have a variety of intelligences. These can be used to carry out at least seven forms of analysis: 1) linguistic (writer, poet), 2) logical-mathematical (scientist), 3) musical (composer), 4) spatial (architect), 5) kinesthetic (athlete, dancer), 6) interpersonal (teacher), 7) intrapersonal (self-knowledge).[4] Depending on which kind of intelligence predominates in a person, that person will perceive certain aspects of a problem with greater clarity than another. Appreciating the diversity of intellectual endowments during consultation permits us to be receptive to all perspectives and actively seek out everyone's contribution.

Furthermore, each of us has unique life experiences as well as a predominating virtue that influences the way we perceive and interpret the events around us. Some may see every matter through the 'lens of justice,' while the 'lens of mercy' may color others' views. The psychologist, Abraham Maslow, is attributed with the well-known saying, "When the only tool you have is a hammer, you tend to see every problem as a nail." If we do not consult with others whose ways of perceiving are different, it is easy to think that our point of view encompasses the whole truth. However, by listening carefully to a diversity of outlooks and attempting to understand how others see the situation, we broaden our understanding and attain a fuller comprehension of reality.

If we remember that different ideas simply reflect different aspects of a larger truth, we will encourage all participants to share their thoughts with complete freedom and give full expression to the dictates of their consciences. This attitude allows us to search for the truth contained in each idea, creatively combine it with the truth found in other perspectives, and arrive at a final decision that far surpasses any of the original contributions.

▶ Effective Listening

For diverse views to effectively inform the emerging truth, we must create an environment that welcomes differing opinions, no matter how much they may clash, recognizing that they are necessary for the process. This requires good *listening* skills and a sincere desire to understand diverse perspectives. It calls for humility and an *attitude of learning* — an attitude that is only likely to occur in a loving, united atmosphere. When such an atmosphere exists and all participants are committed to truth and justice, the group often shows surprising creativity, coming up with innovative ideas that would never have occurred to any of the participants acting alone. In this rarefied atmosphere, the members often remark that the authentic interaction of the group resulted in dramatic insights and leaps of understanding quite distinct from the initial ideas that they brought to the meeting.

The capacity to truly hear another point of view is a skill that can be taught and learned. It requires practice and patience. It implies quieting internal commentary when someone else is speaking and refraining from the temptation to formulate a rebuttal to an opposing point of view. Quieting the internal "chatter" takes practice but is necessary in order to really hear another person. It requires focusing our full attention on understanding, feeling, and even experiencing what is being said rather than the emotions that someone else's words evoke in us. If we focus on our subjective reactions, we become pre-occupied with our own vulnerabilities rather than on the real issues being discussed and on the exploration of truth. To be good listeners, we must suspend all judgment, release biases, and acknowledge that our own understanding is only partial. Above all, we must be vigilant that we are responding authentically to the issues at hand and not to emotions that the issues evoke in us. This process demands humility and faith that the outcome will be a greater measure of justice for all — justice that will uphold everyone's rights including our own. Exercises to practice this important skill can greatly improve our capacity to learn from differing points of view.

▶ Seeking Justice

The significance of this approach to decision-making is reinforced when we understand the process of consultation as "the operating expression of justice in human affairs."[5] Once consultation has helped us to understand the truth of a situation, we commit ourselves to upholding justice as our guiding principle when trying to determine the wisest course of action. Furthermore, we realize that the consultative process itself tends to lead to more just decisions than those made through other means. When only one person (or even a group of like-minded people lacking diversity) makes a decision, it is easy to overlook some ways in which that decision may affect others. However, when the consultation involves a diverse group of people, who may be affected in different ways by the decision, all parties have the opportunity to present their perspectives, so that the group can try to understand them and take them into account. As a result, it is less likely that a decision may unwittingly, or even consciously, be the cause of injustice towards a particular person or group.

Another factor that contributes to just decisions is the awareness of the reciprocal relationship that exists between the well-being of the entire human family and the well-being of each individual and group within that whole. Solving our problems by passing them on to another group will ultimately cause even greater problems for us and for our group, whereas considering the well-being of others, no matter how remote they may seem, will redound to our own well-being. If we recognize the organic oneness of all humanity, if we have expansive love, we will need to consider the effects of our decisions, not only on ourselves or our interest groups, but also on other groups, organizations, communities, countries, and even humankind as a whole.

▶ QUALITIES ESSENTIAL FOR CONSULTATION

It is easier to broaden our understanding of the truth and to make wise, just decisions through consultation when we practice the following qualities:

1) *Sincerity and purity of motive.* We desire to understand more of the truth and not simply impose our own ideas or favor our own personal interests.

2) *Radiance of spirit.* We display a friendly and receptive demeanor and are optimistic and enthusiastic. We look for the positive elements in every idea.

3) *Detachment.* Once we have contributed an idea, we consider that it belongs to the group and do not get upset if others change it or offer opposing ideas. Rather, we pursue any modifications needed, even rejection or going in a completely different direction.

4) *Commitment to truth.* We are passionate about the search for

truth and are committed to applying principles, such as unity, truthfulness, and justice.

5) *Modesty and humility.* We do not boast or try to put ourselves above others. We recognize that our understanding is limited.

6) *Patience.* If it is hard to reach a decision, we keep calm. We do not complain about others. Neither do we accept an unsuitable decision just because we are tired.

7) *Spirit of service.* We are collaborators and willingly offer to help with whatever needs to be done.

Of course, consultation is a process that is carried out by real human beings in the real world. Interactions are not magically freed from the impact of factors such as emotion, manipulation, power-seeking, egotism, prejudice, personal preference, and the perception of dominance due to personality or gender. Such conditions have long contributed to the conflicts and injustices that are manifested in the world. This is precisely why those who aspire to demonstrate transformative leadership are called upon to develop the qualities needed for effective consultation — to champion new methods of collective inquiry and to achieve consensus in practical situations while solving problems and promoting progress, despite human fallibility.

▶ Unity in Consultation

Consultation is most productive when we maintain a spirit of unity, while allowing for full and frank discussion of ideas, including the clash of differing opinions. Without this overarching spirit of unity, disagreement with our ideas may be misinterpreted as personal attacks, leaving us feeling resentful and defensive. When we feel anger or resentment towards other participants, we cannot consider their ideas dispassionately and we become blind to their perspectives. This disrupts the search for truth, thwarting the purpose of consultation. Therefore, we must be careful not to personalize rejection of our ideas.

If we have an ongoing problem with another participant, we need to resolve our hard feelings or misunderstandings outside the consultative session. Only then can we approach the consultation in the spirit needed for it to succeed. Unity implies much more than the lack of negative feelings. It entails a positive, cordial, and appreciative attitude among the members of the group. This is best achieved when we cultivate close relationships with the other members both outside as well as within meetings, thereby nurturing a spirit of appreciation, sincerity and warmth in our interactions.

During the meeting, we can each monitor our behavior so that the ways in which we express ourselves contribute both to the search for truth and to a spirit of unity. The following guidelines can help us to do so:

1) presenting our ideas with clarity, courtesy, dignity, and moderation;

2) sharing what our conscience dictates, even when we fear that no one else will understand or accept what we say;

3) showing detachment from our ideas, clarifying them if necessary, but avoiding stubborn insistence that others must accept them;

4) treating others' opinions with respect — listening with empathy and the genuine desire to be educated about their point of view, without ever mocking, deprecating, or ridiculing any person or idea;

5) avoiding anger or distress when others present contrary ideas or seem to disregard our contributions.

Unity is both the foundation of consultation and its fruit. It must be cultivated before, during, and after consultation. Although consultation endeavors to reach decisions based on unanimous agreement, sometimes it is not possible to resolve a difference of opinion. It is then necessary to decide by voting and accept the decision of the majority. When the decision is not unanimous, it is essential that those who were not in agreement support the decision, cooperate in implementing it, and refrain from criticism. By supporting the decision, unity is preserved. If the decision turns out to be wrong, over time all will come to realize that it was erroneous and together will be able to change it. On the other hand, if those who were not in agreement with the decision complain about it and refuse to support it, and then it fails, it will cause greater disunity. Those who were against the decision will feel smug about being right and those who were in favor of the decision will complain that it failed because of criticism and lack of support. The truth will never be known. The disunity generated by the disagreement will discourage the group from future collaboration.

Consultation is a necessary tool for imperfect people in an imperfect world. Although it does require a measure of internal effort and restraint, it is a process that has been learned and implemented successfully worldwide among various nations and cultures, educated and illiterate, rich and poor, powerful and oppressed.

The capability of participating effectively in consultation is a key to the process of collective transformation at all levels, from the family to international organizations. It is also a prerequisite for the practice of many other capabilities of transformative leadership, such as: promoting unity in diversity, creating a shared vision, transforming dominating relationships, establishing justice, and practicing transformative leadership in the family.

PROMOTING UNITY IN DIVERSITY

We might appreciate why unity is important for collective decision-making, but when speaking of the need for the unity of humankind, a common objection is that unification is impossible due to the great diversity of the peoples of the world. It is one thing to create unity in a small gathering of people working to solve a common problem, but unity in the world may sound utopian. This objection is the result of a mental model that confuses unity with uniformity and diversity with division.

To understand the origin of this error, it is useful to differentiate three stages in the social evolution of humanity. The first was *unity in uniformity*, in which social cohesion was maintained through the imposition of the same way of thinking and acting, such as occurs in tribal and traditional societies. The second was *division in diversity*, in which different factions struggled to break out of the standardized way of looking at things and defend their individuality, a stage that characterizes most of the world today. The third stage, which we are presently entering, is *unity in diversity*, in which the richness of human diversity is preserved and coordinated through unifying principles.

In today's world the first two models lead to conflict. When *unity in uniformity* exists, conformity is imposed from above, requiring that members adhere to the group's ways of thinking and acting. When *division in diversity* exists, differences lead to the separation of people into social classes, political parties, sects, and factions, and to constant struggles among them. As a result, society is weakened by sectarianism. In contrast, peace results from striving to model our ways of thinking, acting, and organizing ourselves upon the principle of *unity in diversity* among ethnic groups, cultures, s, ideologies, and political and economic systems.

Unlike the previous models that promote conflict, the world today must progress to this third stage of development. Neither cultural imperialism, that seeks uniformity by making everyone else submit to its standards, nor exaggerated ethnocentrism, that aspires to turn each culture into a separate country, are suitable for our present-day world where ever-increasing travel and migration continually bring us into contact with a diversity of cultures with whom we need to interact productively. Only the practice of unity in diversity can simultaneously honor the identity and dignity of each cultural group and promote genuine appreciation and harmonious relationships among them.

The need for *unity in diversity* is not limited, however, to relationships among people of different cultures. We also need to practice it in our relationships with those of different professions, since the professional world is hampered by excessive specialization. Different disciplines are often isolated from one another by professional jargon that can be as incomprehensible to the non-initiated as a foreign language. None of these specialties by itself, however, is able to solve the serious problems that afflict humanity today. We can only make progress in the solution of many of these problems if professionals from different disciplines learn to practice *unity in diversity*, working together with an interdisciplinary focus. This combined effort will only be effective if it is characterized by mutual appreciation, sincere attempts to understand what each discipline can offer, and cooperative, coordinated work.

We also need to practice *unity in diversity* in the family, to safeguard the individuality and creativity of its members. This implies that husband and wife encourage one another and their children to cultivate their own creativity, interests and friends. By doing so, they will more fully develop their particular talents and capabilities. They will be more fulfilled in life, happier, more capable and have more to bring to family relationships. Without respect for diversity and warm support for the individuality of each family member, unity can degenerate into static, suffocating uniformity. As a result, the couple may become disrespectful of and bored with one another while the children become rebellious.

To prevent diversity from degenerating into indifference and divisiveness, family members need to consult frequently and transparently about their plans, needs, feelings and desires. As they build unity and trust, they express love by spontaneously sharing their lives and aspirations with other members. They reciprocate that love by showing interest in what the others have shared and even by accompanying one another in their individual activities when invited. Transparent, frequent consultation and sharing are keys to fostering unity in the home and elsewhere.

The world around us offers abundant examples of *unity in diversity*. The human body is the most highly differentiated and specialized biological organism that exists. In spite of this, all of its parts, organs and systems function in perfect harmony when it is in good health. Beautiful music is achieved by the harmonious combination of a great number of instruments, tones, rhythms, notes, chords and progressions. In an ecosystem, unity in diversity is essential to guaranteeing the well-being of each species. In an economic system it is necessary for maintaining the stability of the market. In government, the federal system respects local autonomy while regulating relationships among states and other agencies.

We can use these examples to identify the principles implied by *unity in diversity*:

    1) Each one of the diverse elements is necessary and important.

Diversity is not merely a problem to be tolerated, but is critical to the harmonious functioning of the whole.

2) Cooperation and coordination serve as integrating factors among the elements.

3) The well-being of each part and the well-being of the whole have a reciprocal relationship, each contributing to the other.

4) The integrated whole is far more competent and powerful than the sum of its parts.

5) When we consider the creation of *unity in diversity* among people, two more operational principles come into play:

- The foundation for unity is agreement on basic ethical principles to guide action.

- The best solutions come from group consultation, with its implications of searching for truth and promoting justice and well-being for all.

Since the practice of *unity in diversity* is new for most of us, we need to consciously cultivate attitudes that contribute to it, appreciating — even celebrating — differences, opening ourselves to new ideas, and tolerating ambiguity during the process of achieving a unified understanding. Moreover, we have to resist attitudes that obstruct unity, such as prejudices and attachment to our own ideas. When we achieve this kind of unity, there is nothing we cannot overcome or achieve.

CHAPTER VII

CAPABILITIES FOR

SOCIAL TRANSFORMATION

ESTABLISHING JUSTICE

The foundation of social order is justice. To act justly implies giving each person or institution what is rightfully deserved. Economic justice implies taking into account the quality and quantity of work done, as well as the person's needs. In some contexts this implies equality — giving everyone the same treatment — for example, equal pay for equal work. However, in other situations, justice implies equity — giving differentiated treatment based on specific needs — for example, giving special assistance to those who are handicapped, and not to others.

Social justice implies:

1) elimination of exploitation and of extremes of wealth and poverty;

2) equilibrium between individual rights and the collective good;

3) just social structures and authorities — choosing public officials and leaders based on criteria of capacity and merit, free
from the influence of politics, relationship, or money; and

4) establishment and impartial application of a system of reasonable laws, in which all are subject to the law and nobody
is "above the law."

The establishment of social justice also implies freeing people from
oppression. Oppression exploits ignorance: 1) ignorance of the universal principles upon which justice is based, 2) ignorance of the laws
and institutions that people may call on when treated unjustly, and
3) ignorance of the skills that can facilitate escape from an oppressive
situation. Education focused on emancipating people from this triple
ignorance provides the tools to free them from oppression.

In striving to establish social justice, we need to exemplify justice in our daily lives and also employ just methods in our struggle.
Unfortunately, at times we see great champions of social justice who
use their positions for personal gain, are dishonest, show favoritism,
discriminate against women or minorities, or misrepresent those they
oppose. This lack of coherence between words and deeds frustrates the
achievement of the very goal they so vociferously proclaim. Rather,
the creation of a just society begins with the practice of justice in our
individual lives and organizations, by making decisions and taking
actions based on principles, rather than on our own personal or sectarian interests.

To act with justice, we must first strive to eliminate every trace of
prejudice, since prejudice clouds our vision and warps our judgment.
To overcome prejudice, we must be committed to the unfettered *investigation of truth*. If we continually base our decisions on what we have
perceived with our own eyes and have discerned through our own anal-

ysis and reflection, applying the most elevated principles that we know, we will discover that prejudices are based on stereotypes that do not apply universally to any group. We will be able to evaluate the merits of each situation more dispassionately and base our decisions on evidence. Our resulting actions are then much more likely to be just.

No matter how deeply we reflect, however, our points of view are always limited since we tend to focus on some aspects of an issue and ignore others. To gain a more comprehensive understanding, we can proactively elicit diverse perspectives through group consultation. This will broaden our understanding of an issue, facilitating our perception of aspects that are important to others. This kind of collective inquiry is essential for making just decisions characterized by a true equilibrium between the well-being of the whole and the well-being of each of the parts.

Both individual reflection and group consultation are critical in determining a just division of the rights and responsibilities that are implicit in any relationship. We must guard against focusing primarily on *our* rights and others' responsibilities and give equal importance to *their* rights and our responsibilities.

While it is essential that we investigate truth as extensively as we can, there comes a moment when we must make a decision and act, even when we are not certain that the decision is correct. This requires both courage and willingness to take responsibility for the consequences of our actions. We have to accept that we may make mistakes and take action to rectify them when they occur.

Injustice is easy to recognize if we are the victims of oppression. In standing up to injustice and oppression directed at us, it is important to do so calmly, while insisting on fair treatment. When injustice is directed at someone else, it is sometimes not so easy to recognize. Or if we recognize it, we may not be as motivated to confront it. Sometimes it is easier to look the other way, rationalizing that, "things have always been that way and are not going to change." However, if we are to be true champions of justice, we have to raise our voices, even at personal cost, no matter where injustice occurs. Defending justice is not optional if we aspire to transformative leadership. Without justice, unity is impossible, and without unity, we cannot achieve anything of lasting value.

TRANSFORMING DOMINATING RELATIONSHIPS

As human civilization has become increasingly interconnected, the dynamics of organizational and interpersonal relationships have become more complex. Countless examples that demonstrate the ineffectiveness of aggressive competition in today's interdependent world compel a deeper exploration of approaches conducive to collaboration. One way of understanding the implications of collaboration is to examine the dominant cultural assumptions underlying individual and organizational relationships. In Chapter II, we discussed the dynamic interplay between assumptions we make about human nature and about society and how one reinforces the other. If we see human nature as purely self-serving and society as a competitive jungle, then we will view all our relationships through that lens and behave accordingly.

▶ POWER

To better understand the implications of the assumptions we make, it is helpful to examine power and its dynamics. Michael Karlberg explains that there are various ways to conceptualize power. In its broadest definition, power is seen as *capacity* to achieve certain results. *Adversarial power relations* arise from a competitive mental model whereas *mutualistic power relations* result from a focus on cooperation.[1]

(from Michael Karlberg)

ADVERSARIAL RELATIONS 'power against' competition		MUTUALISTIC RELATIONS 'power with' cooperation	
INEQUALITY 'power over'	EQUALITY 'balance of power'	INEQUALITY 'assisted empowerment'	EQUALITY 'mutual empowerment'
coercion domination oppression	stalemate compromise frustration	education nurturance assistance	synergy collaboration coordination
win/lose	lose/lose	(win)/win	win/win

Karlberg further analyzes the different dynamics of power and explores what happens in relationships, depending on whether there is equal or unequal power between the parties involved. In adversarial relationships, when there is unequal power, one party exercises *power over* the other, in which case one person's will dominates and determines the course of action, while the other is powerless and at the mercy of the one in power. The result is coercion, domination and oppression. In this case the party with more power *wins* and the other party *loses*.

If the power dynamics are equal in an adversarial relationship, there is a *balance of power*. Each party tries to exert power over the other, but because the power struggle is between equals, neither is successful. As a result, both feel frustrated and reach a stalemate since neither party is willing to budge. As a result, it becomes impossible to come to an agreement or take action. Sometimes through negotiation both may grudgingly give up something that they value in order to reach an agreement, but neither is really satisfied. In this case, both *lose*.

In mutualistic relations, however, whether there is equality or inequality of power, both parties *win*. Mutualistic relationships with inequality of power are characteristic of parent/child or student/mentor relationships. In these cases, the party with greater power assists the development of those with lesser power by teaching, encouraging and accompanying them, in order to help them develop their capabilities. Karlberg calls this *assisted empowerment*. The more powerful benefits by witnessing the fruits of capacity building, while the less powerful develop capabilities to prepare them for equal power relations in the future. Mutualistic relationships with equality of power — relationships between true equals — are characterized by collaboration, coordination and synergy. Both achieve more by working together than the sum of what they could achieve working individually. The result is *mutual empowerment*, in which both parties *win*. When the foundation of the relationship is mutualistic, what may begin as assisted empowerment may quickly result in mutual empowerment. A relationship may seem unequal initially and one party may have more formal power, as occurs in a position of authority or when one has greater knowledge or experience. However, the trust and encouragement inherent in such a relationship helps the one with less power to quickly develop his unique capabilities so that within a short time, a complementary relationship between equals is formed.

In brief, mutualistic power relations form the foundation for *collaboration* and free people from the oppression of domination. A family, organization, community, nation, or world characterized by mutualistic relationships empowers all of the participants, generates synergy and creates an environment in which all can prosper.

However, a shift from the adversarial power relations prevalent in society to mutualistic relations geared toward service to the common good implies transforming the antiquated *mental model* of domination into a *conceptual framework* of mutually supportive relationships. It requires letting go of pre-conceived ideas and expectations, critically examining assumptions, being receptive to a more comprehensive view of reality, and embracing with an open mind and heart a new conceptual framework – one that will allow us to productively engage in group consultation. Such a framework facilitates collaboration and accelerates progress.

▶ Building a New Conceptual Framework of Mutuality

To gain clarity on what this transformation implies, we must first identify the assumptions that underlie the mental model of domination as well as those principles that support the conceptual framework of mutually supportive relationships. Dominating relationships are based on a mental model with faulty assumptions, such as:

1) Some people are superior to others.

2) It is permissible to use power to impose our will on another.

3) Irreconcilable differences will always lead to conflict, especially when there are limited resources.

4) Domination is inevitable. What can vary is who dominates and the degree and type of domination.

Relationships of reciprocity and mutual benefit are based on a conceptual framework with a systemic focus on *interdependence*. The principles underlying this framework are:

1) Unity in diversity is a source of power and contributes to well-being for all.

2) A common vision and agreement on fundamental ethical and moral principles strengthen unity.

3) Justice is a prerequisite for abiding unity.

4) Sharing and mutual service strengthen unity far beyond that which can be achieved by justice alone.

5) Differences that arise from diversity can be resolved through group consultation.

Transformation implies an irreversible, qualitative change toward something better. The transformation of a mental model into a conceptual framework that supports mutualistic relationships implies a transformation of our thought processes — a change in the way we perceive and understand the world. This, in turn, is manifested in transformation of our attitudes and behaviors.

A workshop can be an ideal situation in which to critically scrutinize the mental model of dominating relationships and to explore the conceptual framework of mutually supportive relationships. In such an environment, the participants are open to learning, develop the skill of analyzing unexamined assumptions, and are receptive to new ways of viewing reality. We will go into greater detail about how this can be done when discussing the capability of "Empowering Education." However, we often need to work through this process by ourselves in real life situations, where we have customarily dominated certain people or been dominated by them. In such cases, we may want to utilize the *ladder of inference* as a tool to help us understand the root causes of our mental models and resulting behaviors, leading to their transformation. This tool is explained in detail in Chapter V. Once we clearly understand and are committed to the new conceptual framework, we face the challenging task of applying it in all of our relationships.

Sincere reflection on our previously unexamined assumptions may lead us to discover that in some relationships we are dominating. If we then try to modify our behavior in order to transform the relationship into one that is mutually supportive, we should not be surprised if at first there is lack of receptivity. Passivity and distrust are learned defenses. Therefore, we will probably need to explain the 'new rules of the game,' facilitate the development of capabilities such as *consultation* and the promotion of *unity in diversity*, and assist others to assume new responsibilities. We will also need to ensure that we model behaviors consistent with mutually supportive relationships in order to build trust and catalyze transformation in the relationship.

If we have been dominated in a relationship with a particular person, it is even more challenging to transform that relationship. Some positive lines of action include: basing our actions on principles, standing up to the dominating person without taking a spiteful attitude, respecting his rights so that we do not change roles and become the dominator, and seeking peaceful solutions to conflicts. Mahatma Gandhi and Martin Luther King have demonstrated the effectiveness of confronting social injustice in this way. On the individual level, the practice of non-confrontational conflict resolution emphasizes the same principles.

It is important to understand that domination and submission are two sides of the same coin. Often a man who is dominated in his job returns home and dominates his wife. She, in turn, dominates the children. This implies that the culprit is not the person who dominates in a particular relationship (since in other situations, that same person is dominated); rather it is the mental model of dominating relationships. Consequently, transforming dominating relationships does not imply overthrowing the person who is dominating, since that would only change who is dominating, but not the type of relationship that exists.

▶ DEVELOPING COLLABORATIVE RELATIONSHIPS

The only true way to overcome domination is by learning to actively promote collaborative relationships. We can begin by changing our behaviors in the role over which we have the most control – that in which we are the dominator. Based on that experience, it will be easier to transform those relationships in which we have been dominated.

Successfully practicing this capability implies that we fully recognize our interdependence. Working in collaboration with a diversity of people requires a level of trust and goodwill that is inconsistent with the prevailing world-view in our society. Thus, if we wish to engage in collaborative efforts that contribute to social transformation, we need to embrace a world-view based on the organic oneness and interdependence of humankind, recognizing that our very survival depends upon our seeing and embracing the new paradigm — *humanity constitutes one human family and one race with a collective heritage and a common destiny.* Suffering and injustice in any part affect the whole. We can no more distance ourselves from the problems in our society and the world as a whole than the human body can distance itself from a painful body part. If we wish to commit ourselves to collaboration as a way of life, we need to recognize that our individual well-being is intimately connected to our collective well-being.

In particular, we need to develop a growing awareness of the importance of *diversity.* In most of the world, diversity is either a source of conflict or it is tolerated – perhaps even accepted. We need to go beyond that and appreciate the richness it adds to our understanding and *celebrate* it, welcome it, encourage it, and promote it, recognizing it as a precious resource for offering us a broader understanding of reality. One way of welcoming diversity is to develop effective listening skills. Nothing is more encouraging to those who are expressing their precious ideas than receiving the full attention of another person and witnessing his genuine interest. When we focus open-hearted attention on another human being, it is a powerful magnet for achieving unity. This attitude of mutual appreciation leads to collective learning and creates *unity in diversity* – the foundation for effective collaboration.

EMPOWERING EDUCATION

Empowering education prepares people to transform their lives and their communities. We outlined the steps such an educational process requires in the introduction to this book: *providing context, challenging mental models, transforming our understanding through critical analysis, adopting a new conceptual framework, forming a learning community* and *taking action.* We referred to this as *transformative learning* as opposed to informative learning. These steps are not necessarily sequential; they may even at times be simultaneous. But it is important for us to be aware that they exist and, as educators, address them. *Providing context* ensures that the participants in an educational activity see the relevance of the information for their lives.

Challenging mental models, transforming our understanding through critical analysis and adopting a new conceptual framework are closely interrelated. The process of deconstructing mental models, often leads to 'disorienting dilemmas,' as the participants ask themselves, "If what I have always believed is not true or beneficial, then what?" This important step is a prelude to the transformation of understanding, opening the mind on a deep level to explore new alternatives. Thus, we need to devise activities that help the members of the group grapple with the problematic aspects of a topic in order to help them weed out correct from incorrect assumptions and develop a true understanding of how a certain aspect of life operates. This allows them to explore the subject matter from different angles and to integrate it with previous knowledge so that they can apply what they are learning to their lives.

▶ Workshops

Teaching this process is best accomplished in a participatory workshop. This kind of education cannot be communicated fully in a book or in a lecture format. The participants must work with the information, test it out, apply it, consult about it, see the results, and then plan further action.

One element that is often missing in educational activities, even in participatory workshops, is helping participants acquire tools that will guide and hone their own learning. These tools help us to gain insight into our own thinking processes and to understand why we behave as we do. Since empowering education implies a transformation of understanding from restrictive ways of thinking to more inclusive perspectives, among the best

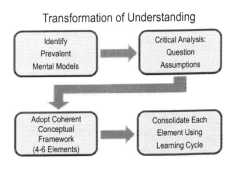

tools we can offer students are the tools for critical analysis that challenge mental models. Initially, we have to guide them through the process of literally "hanging their assumptions" like pictures before them awaiting scrutiny. Then they need to learn to do this for themselves.

In a workshop we use specific activities to guide the participants through the process of challenging mental models, transforming their understanding through critical analysis, and adopting a new conceptual framework. First, we help the participants to identify the prevailing mental models related to the subject matter. An interactive exercise, in which the participants portray or dramatize "what usually happens" in certain situations, is one way of achieving this. Another is to simply ask, "What do most people think of when we mention X?" and then categorize the replies into the most prevalent mental models.

This is then followed by exercises that help the participants to critically analyze and question the mental models that they have identified. In the capability of "Learning from Reflection on Action," we mentioned some tools that are useful for this purpose, such as using the *ladder of inference*, critically analyzing the effects of the mental model on others and society, and identifying internal inconsistencies and logical fallacies, especially in the light of scientific evidence.

Once the participants have heightened their awareness of the fallacies of commonly held mental models and are open to alternatives, we can present a new conceptual framework that is in harmony with scientific evidence and with ethical principles. This framework is most easily remembered and applied when it can be summarized in four to six concrete elements.

Finally, we use successive applications of the learning cycle — with its phases of experience, reflection, conceptualization and application — to consolidate the understanding and application of each element. We discussed one use of the learning cycle in Chapter V—"Learning from Reflection on Action." The cycle is also an effective tool for designing transformative learning sessions. When used for this purpose, the learning session:

1) begins by structuring an experience related to the topic, such as a skit, a short video, or an on-site visit;

2) presents key questions for the participants to consult among themselves about what they have learned from the experience and how it relates to the topic;

3) complements their conclusions with a presentation of key concepts to help them develop a deeper understanding of the topic; and

4) finishes by assigning group work where they apply what they learned through simulations, problem-solving, planning a project, or demonstrating their understanding by use of relevant drawings, diagrams, songs or other artistic expressions.

Each phase of the learning cycle has an important part to play:

1) The *experience* serves to awaken interest and engage the participants.

2) *Reflection* connects that experience with previous knowledge.

3) *Conceptualization* helps participants deepen that knowledge.

4) The all-important phase of *application* gives them the opportunity to practice what they have learned.

The practice then yields a whole new set of experiences that leads to another cycle of learning. Multiple iterations of the learning cycle result in change and growth based on deepened understanding combined with practice.

The learning cycle is useful not only for transforming a mental model into a conceptual framework, but also for achieving ever greater depth of understanding on any topic. Indeed, educational activities based on the four phases of the learning cycle are the easiest and most effective ways to facilitate interactive learning and initiate a process of continual improvement.

▶ A LEARNING COMMUNITY

As we develop our capabilities and apply them to transform our lives and our environments, we need people with whom to consult. In other words, we need to form *a learning community* in which we can test our new capabilities and make adjustments. The community becomes our learning crucible, providing support and accompaniment. One way of structuring this community is by carrying out ongoing educational activities with the same group of participants. The facilitator can then both give guidance and provide feedback as the participants learn to apply their new knowledge in real life situations. As the group matures, 'assisted empowerment' becomes 'mutual empowerment' as all the members learn to provide this feedback to one another.

Of course the development of capabilities for personal and social transformation is a life-long process that needs to be revisited on a daily basis. Recognizing that it is essentially a learning experience that never ends, helps us to be patient with progress in small steps. Developing the habit of self-reflection individually, and of consultation collectively, helps us to reinforce our learning and celebrate movement in the right direction, no matter how small.

To summarize, in designing an empowering educational experience, we must begin with an understanding of the process of transformative learning. Participants then must acquire three very important tools: 1) how to critically analyze mental models, 2) how to design educational activities formatted on the learning cycle, and 3) how to sustain a learning attitude in order to persevere when progress is slow.

ELABORATING A PRINCIPLE-BASED SHARED VISION

A vision is a description of a desired future, challenging but not impossible to achieve, based on shared principles. A clear vision of what we want to accomplish — knowing our destination — contributes to unity of thought and aids in decision-making, clarifying the choice of roads that lead there. On the other hand, as so aptly put by Lewis Carroll, "If you don't know where you are going, any road will get you there."[2] Vision also gives meaning to our daily tasks, since these tasks, however mundane they may be, bring us closer to making our vision a reality.

Any important undertaking, from the construction of a village health center to the establishment of world peace, begins with a vision. The more clearly we see the vision and the more we consult about it with others, the greater will be the clarity of the path leading to its achievement.

Virtually all people tend to respond positively to visions based on noble principles. Consequently, the first step in elaborating a vision capable of inspiring others consists of identifying the principles that will guide the vision. Then, using these principles as a framework, we can elaborate the vision itself. The vision should be simple and clear enough to be easily remembered and concrete enough to provide guidance for action. Such a vision, articulated with clarity and based on noble principles, will invariably attract like-minded people and resources for its achievement.

One systematic method that can be utilized to elaborate a vision with a group uses a matrix such as the one that follows. Although the example is related to education, a similar matrix can be elaborated related to any subject of concern. We do this by identifying principles related to the subject, incorporating those principles implicitly in the list of topics in the left-hand column, and adding other relevant top-ics as they are identified. In the example used, some of the principles implicitly included are:

1) an emphasis on the spiritual as well as the intellectual dimen-sion of the human being (moral education),

2) a focus on cooperation rather than competition (spirit of uni-ty and cooperation; service activities),

3) equal rights and opportunities for boys and girls (gender eq-uity), and

4) an emphasis on the students' process of learning rather than the act of teaching (physical and emotional well being of the students; use of participatory methodologies).

ELABORATION OF A VISION RELATED TO EDUCATION		
TOPIC	What have we achieved to date?	What do we want to have achieved in 3 years?
Physical and Emotional Well- Being of the Students		
Spirit of Unity and Cooperation		
Use of Participatory Methodologies		
Moral Education		
Gender Equity		
Service Activities		
Appreciation of Own Culture and Openness to Other Cultures		

Use of Arts and Music		
Environmental Awareness and Practices		
Involvement of the Educational Community, Especially Parents		

The relevant principles and topics can either be elaborated by a core group beforehand or through consultation with all the participants. For practical purposes, a combination of these approaches often proves most effective: initially presenting topics elaborated by a core group and then giving the participants the opportunity to modify or add topics. Once the first column is fully defined, the participants fill in the rest of the matrix. They then choose three to five items from the last column to form the core of their vision. Finally, they draft the vision in a few short sentences.

A well-elaborated vision serves as a source of guidance. It defines a *north* or "compass point" towards which to orient actions and decisions. Consequently, it indicates priorities in the use of human and material resources. But more importantly, a good vision motivates action. The perception of the gap that exists between the vision and current reality generates tension that can be transformed into creative energy. We can use this energy to take concrete steps toward fulfillment of the vision. The progress achieved will release further energy and fuel our enthusiasm even more. The amount of energy generated by the vision is directly proportional to our commitment to it and our faith that we will achieve it. If the vision does not truly interest us, or if we see little chance of actually achieving it, it cannot energize us. Furthermore, if we do not transform the tension generated by the gap between the vision and current reality into energy that propels us into action, this same tension will become oppressive and may cause us to forsake the vision altogether. This can occur when the vision seems beyond the possibility of achievement, or when we lack clarity about how to attain it.

Vision is important both on personal and institutional levels. In order for an institutional vision to influence its members, they must make it their own. Those who collaborate in formulating a vision are the most likely to identify with it. But we need to ensure that those who did not participate in its formulation become so familiar with the vision that they make a commitment to its achievement. This is most likely to occur when the vision is widely shared and frequently referred to.

Ownership of the vision is facilitated when the members of the organization have opportunities both to consult about it and to participate in activities that reflect it. This participatory process not only helps the members to better understand the vision, it also makes it easier for them to find coherence between their own personal visions and the institutional vision. The closer the coherence, the greater will be their commitment. In fact, since many people do not have a clearly articulated personal vision, as long as the institutional vision is in harmony with their values, they may even formulate their personal visions in light of the more clearly defined institutional vision. Individual capacity to formulate a vision varies, however. Therefore, in order to inspire the members, the institutional vision should be expressed in terms that are lofty, yet simple and comprehensible.

TRANSFORMING INSTITUTIONS

Adoption of an ethical framework for institutional health is gathering increasing support globally. The recognition that institutions have a vital role to play in humanity's collective well-being is underscored by the increasingly urgent call for corporate social responsibility by the public. Successful businesses can no longer turn their backs on environmental and human costs. In fact, more and more focus is centered not only on demanding that businesses protect human rights and adopt environmentally friendly practices, but also that they become proactive in contributing to the betterment of the societies in which they flourish.

In 1999, UN Secretary General, Kofi Annan, launched the United Nations 'Global Compact,' a policy initiative calling on businesses to align their operations with ten universally recognized ethical principles embracing human rights, the work environment, and anti-corruption practices. Its goal is to advance economic and social development in ways that benefit all and contribute to the common good, Some 8,700 corporations and other stakeholders from more than 130 countries have embraced this effort. As such, it is the largest corporate social responsibility initiative in the world.[3]

Some have gone further and called on an expansion of this effort to include other multi-national organizations. Ernst-Ulrich Petersmann, professor of International Law at the European University Institute in Florence, Italy, proposes the additional adoption of a "'Global Compact' between the UN and UN specialized agencies, as well as with other worldwide public organizations such as the World Trade Organization (WTO), so as to integrate universally recognized human rights into the law and practice of intergovernmental organizations... and to engage in transparent dialogues about the contribution by specialized agencies to the promotion and protection of human rights."[4]

The historic precedent of the 'Global Compact,' especially as it evolves, is helping to create worldwide awareness of the importance of adopting an ethical framework for all institutions. As more and more organizations, whether they are businesses, non-governmental organizations, or even local institutions at the community level such as a school or clinic, adopt ethical frameworks for their operations, they will be protected from the adverse consequences of corrupt practices.

For an institution to achieve its potential as a force for progress and true prosperity, it requires:

1. clearly articulated *values, vision* and *mission,*

2. *alignment* in all its initiatives,

3. *capacity building* for all its members, and

4. a *learning orientation.*

▶ VALUES, VISION AND MISSION

By adopting an ethical framework, the institution articulates the *values* that guide its work and the consequences of violating these core values. Such a statement of values must be so widely shared and appropriated that it becomes part of the institutional culture. As a result, when challenges arise, all will be vigilant to adhere to the core values in searching for solutions. The ethical framework protects the institution from moral compromise in times of difficulty and inspires its members to embrace ethical practices in their roles.

The *vision* and *mission* must be inspiring and easily understood. *Vision* expresses a desired future state of the organization. A *mission* is more limited and defines how the institution, or department within it, conceptualizes its *purpose* in the light of the vision. Members of the organization are more likely to embrace the vision and mission if they have opportunities to participate in formulating them or in deciding how they will be implemented.

▶ Alignment

Once the values, vision, and mission are clarified and widely shared, the challenge is to align all initiatives to reflect this so that the work of the organization is coherent and focused. The power to achieve an organization's goals depends on all of its members, not just those in authority. Although the latter determine the direction of the organization, progress depends on the degree to which each member whole-heartedly embraces the organizational vision and works for its realization within the boundaries of an ethical framework. Successful organizations facilitate expression of the talents of their members and, to the degree possible, channel their creativity into organizational activities that are coherent with each person's ideals. This generates commitment in the members that leads to individual fulfillment and institutional achievement.

▶ Capacity Building

A successful organization needs systems that will foster capacity building both for the institution as well as for each member. We each have our own strengths and perform much better when we feel competent and enjoy what we do. Although people are adaptable and can learn new capabilities, the wise organization assigns functions corresponding to each person's talents and appreciates them for their contributions. *Appreciation* is a powerful motivator for achieving excellence and accelerating learning. Giving sincere praise, listening attentively to ideas and carefully considering them, giving members a certain amount of autonomy to resolve problems within their areas of expertise, expanding opportunities for learning, and delegating interesting tasks, are all ways of communicating appreciation for the members in the organization and enhancing their learning.

Other ways an institution can develop the capacity of its members are through *skills training* and *delegation of responsibility*. Skills training can be provided either directly through on the job training, or indirectly by providing access to continuing education. Delegation of responsibility provides opportunity to try out the new skills and should be commensurate with the capabilities and motivation of each member. According to management expert Kenneth Blanchard, there are predictable stages of development for individuals and for teams within an organization. Anticipating these stages proactively and facilitating the development process can accelerate overall learning.[5] As members develop their skills in a particular function, they pass from an initial stage in which they need guidance and a *highly directive* form of supervision, to the next stage in which they need *support*, knowing they can seek consultation or advice when required. As their capabilities increase, they can gradually be included in *participatory* decision-making, until finally they are capable of having certain tasks completely *delegated* to them, where they receive both the responsibility and the authority to act. Effective delegation is based on win-win agreements that benefit both the member and the institution. These work better if desired results, guidelines, available resources, standards for evaluation, and the consequences of good or bad performance are clearly defined in advance.

▶ LEARNING ORIENTATION

When all the members of an institution are engaged in ongoing training, consultation, and the assumption of new responsibilities, the organization itself becomes a *learning organization*. In a learning organization, communication and suggestions flow in all directions, not only from top to bottom, but also from bottom to top and horizontally as well. In this way, everyone learns from everyone else. In such an organization people are empowered to give their best and most creative output. When taking initiative, some mistakes are inevitable. Such mistakes will not be identified as failures, but rather, as learning opportunities. A mistake that in a hierarchical organization might be a cause of fear, in a learning organization is merely viewed as a challenge that accelerates growth and leads to continuous improvement. When we apply these practices, not only do we unleash the talents of all members of the institution and facilitate innovation, but we also help the organization itself to mature.

UNDERSTANDING HISTORICAL PERSPECTIVE

Knowing the history of our country, culture, or religion and feeling pride in its achievements gives us a sense of identity and encourages cooperation. Nourishing our souls with stories of our forebears' noble deeds strengthens our identity and enkindles within us the desire to emulate them. Historical knowledge also contributes to our understanding of the present, enables us to make distinctions between essential and accidental aspects of our culture, and aids us in understanding the dynamics that have shaped current practices. Knowledge about where we stand from a historical perspective creates a more inclusive context for us to understand who we are and where we are headed.

When we reflect on the long periods involved in the historical trajectory of a people, we obtain a more realistic perspective of what we can expect to achieve in a limited project of two or three years. We become conscious of the need for understanding and patience when our efforts yield only limited results. We become vigilant about aiming our efforts in the right direction, so that, when combined with many other such efforts, transformation may occur. Moreover, this perspective helps us to understand the importance of working with children and youth who will be the leaders of tomorrow.

Frequently, the study of history has been distorted and used to promote exaggerated patriotism characterized by hatred of other peoples. Therefore, we must consider *universality* as an important element in a historical conceptual framework. One test of the universality of any given approach to history is its acceptance by historians from different countries and cultures. We can also evaluate the value of the approach by the degree to which it aids in the perception of patterns in history that are universally significant.

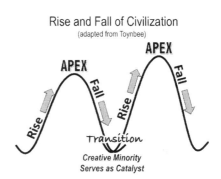

Rise and Fall of Civilization
(adapted from Toynbee)

▶ RISE AND FALL OF CIVILIZATION

Universal historical approaches help us to understand the dynamics of history and to make sense out of current events today. Arnold Toynbee, a British historian, has helped to contribute to this understanding of universal historical processes. His *A Study of History*[6] consists of a 10-volume scrutiny of 23 civilizations in which he analyzes the processes that influence their rise and fall. He concludes that a new civilization arises whenever there exists a series of challenges to which the society responds effectively, inspired by the vision of a creative minority that guides the society in meeting those challenges. On the other hand, a civilization gradually falls into decline when vision is lost and a dominant minority attempts to impose its will by force.

▶ SOCIAL EVOLUTION

Most people view history as a series of random events without any particular relationship one to the other. In 1943, Shoghi Effendi provided an analysis of historic events in terms of humanity's collective learning.[7] Each successful collective learning milestone permitted increasingly complex levels of social organization from family to city-state to nation and now to a global society. He compared the advancement of social organization throughout history to the stages of growth in a human being, who passes from infancy to childhood, then adolescence, and finally attains maturity. More recently, the evolutionary biologist Elisabet Sahtouris has similarly compared human social organization to the same maturation process.[8] According to this analogy, humanity is now in the turbulent stage of adolescence, struggling to achieve the stage of maturity when it will have recognized its interdependence, devised mechanisms for cooperation and developed means to address the various crises confronting it. The outcome will be a planetary society increasingly based on justice, unity and cooperation.

Viewing our current global challenges from these two perspectives, we can see how a creative minority with this historical understanding and a clear vision of humanity's potential state of maturity can provide the leadership to respond to the grave challenges confronting humanity at this critical time. Transformative leadership seeks to develop men and women who will become part of that creative minority.

> *Never doubt that a small group of thoughtful, committed citizens can change the world; indeed, it's the only thing that ever has.*[9]
>
> — *Margaret Mead*

CHAPTER VIII

INTEGRATING THE CAPABILITIES

TRANSFORMATIVE LEADERSHIP IN THE FAMILY

As the smallest social unit, the family serves as an ideal laboratory and *learning community* where we can develop and practice transformative leadership. In the family, we have our most intimate, ongoing relationships. As a result, the weaknesses we manage to cover up in our social relations often come to light in our family life. This painful reality can inspire us to work on the development of those capabilities that will offset our weaknesses, provided that we are committed to our own personal transformation. The tolerance that the family generally has for our mistakes and idiosyncrasies also gives us the opportunity to experiment with new behaviors with less apprehension about how well we do, the mistakes we may make, or our initial awkwardness when we try something new. In this way it serves as a crucible for experimentation.

> *The achievement of full equality between the sexes is one of the most important, though less acknowledged prerequisites of peace. The denial of such equality perpetrates an injustice against one-half of the world's population and promotes in men harmful attitudes and habits that are carried from the family to the workplace, to political life, and ultimately to international relations.*[1]

An even more important reason for us to practice capabilities of transformative leadership in the family is that the dynamics of family relationships generally serve as a model that is repeated in our relationships at work, in society, and even in the international sphere. For example, if we are accustomed to dominating other members of the family or submitting to their domination at home, we will tend to dominate and/or submit to domination at work and in society. Conversely, if at home we learn to practice consultation, to appreciate unity in diversity, and to develop mutually supportive relationships, we will very likely apply these capabilities at work and in society.

▶ A Learning Workshop

Each member of the family has ample opportunities to develop the capabilities of transformative leadership. As parents help their children in this learning process, the children become more responsible, improve their interpersonal relationships, take charge of their own learning, and become more loving members of the family. It also assists the parents to focus their own attention on these capabilities and to be more conscientious in their efforts to practice them.

Basing family life on principles such as truthfulness, cooperation, consultation, and justice, helps children to learn to manage their affairs and responsibilities with *rectitude of conduct*. This requires that parents talk about these principles with children in understandable terms. It also requires that the parents themselves provide good role models, so that their children will learn how to put these principles into practice. The joint elaboration of a *covenant of shared responsibilities*, in which the responsibilities of each family member are stipulated in writing, contributes to an awareness of the diverse rights and responsibilities of each person. It lets children know concretely what is expected of them and helps them to take responsibility for their actions. It also serves as a guide to *justice* within family relationships.

When children have creative ideas, parents can help them to develop the capability of *taking initiative*. They can guide them step by step through the seven phases of initiative and explain the importance of each phase as they come to it — from intention (step 1) through bringing the idea to fruition (step 7). As the children are guided through each step, they learn for themselves what is involved in accomplishing a great task. Parents have the very important role of accompanying their children through this process and modeling what it means to take initiative by defining purpose, elaborating a plan and a schedule, making a commitment, and *persevering* in the face of difficulty, until the results are obtained.

Parents can accelerate learning in any area for their children by assisting them to develop the capability of learning from *reflection on action*. In their role as guides, they can ask questions to help their children learn from their experiences and learn how they might have greater success the next time they attempt something similar. They can teach children to *think systemically* by diagramming with their children how one thing affects another.

Parents can structure family life to also promote the development of interpersonal capabilities by helping their children to become more loving and by creating a safe environment where all can contribute to a more harmonious atmosphere in the home.

▶ Practicing Capabilities Through Games and Activities

Traditional games promote competition, resulting in win/lose outcomes, whereas cooperative games and activities result in joy and the feeling of accomplishment for all. These simple cooperative games are one means of helping all members of the family to enjoy collective activities and focus on the capabilities of *imbuing one's thoughts and actions with love* and of *encouragement*. For example, at the beginning of a family meeting, each member can comment on something that others did during the previous week that he particularly liked.

Parents can promote the use of *consultation* in the home as a means for making decisions and for solving problems. In the process, they can gradually explain the guidelines and qualities that lead to more productive consultation. They can foster appreciation for *unity in diversity* among the different family members, as well as guests or workers in the home, by showing appreciation for the interests and talents of each person. They can demonstrate the power of *encouragement* to release talents in service to the family and the community. Together, these practices help to *transform dominating relationships* within the family into mutually supportive ones.

Parents can inspire in their children the aspiration to contribute to social transformation. For example, telling children stories about cultural heroes reinforces their identity and helps them to acquire a *historical perspective*. They can also work together to *formulate a family mission* towards which all can strive.

Family meetings are a natural way of incorporating the development of many of these capabilities into family life. In these meetings the whole family can discuss problems and responsibilities and plan enjoyable family activities. They can also consult about particular capabilities of transformative leadership and how to better apply them. Furthermore, parents can program a certain amount of individualized time with each child, listening, talking, and sharing activities that the child enjoys. This focused time assures each child of the parents' love. It also gives the child more self-confidence and generates a greater desire to please the parents by developing capabilities the parents consider important.

Making the home into a workshop that nurtures the talents and catalyzes leadership capabilities in each member gives rise not only to enlightened individuals, but also to a transformed family — a social force in the community and potentially in the world, serving the common good.

EPILOGUE

A WORD ABOUT AMBITION

Who Is Superior? [1]

A Master was surprised to hear shouting and altercation going on in his courtyard. When he was told that one of his disciples was at the centre of it, he had the man sent for and asked what the cause of the din was.

"There is a delegation of scholars that has come to visit you. I told them you do not waste your time on men whose heads are stuffed with books and thoughts but devoid of wisdom. These are the people who, in their conceit, create dogmas and divisions among people everywhere."

The Master smiled. "How true, how true," he murmured. "But tell me, is not your conceit in claiming to be different from the scholars the cause of this present conflict and division?"

We have explored the hidden, inner dimensions of *transformative leadership*, and perhaps some of us have begun to apply the guidance, exercises, workshops and techniques presented. We have come to realize that true leadership is far more than application of power, or having charisma, eloquence, a persuasive style, or a magnetic personality. To the extent that we apply this learning in our lives, we will progress toward becoming deeply rooted, sturdy trees that will blossom and bear fruit as our capacities and talents develop and mature. This is a truly epic journey for each of us, for it will last our entire lifetime.

This voyage is fraught with challenges, frustrations, and difficulties — all great, strengthening opportunities that will result in our ability to withstand the turbulent storms that we all must face in life. At many points along this journey, we will see glorious results and develop even more yearning to improve our inner strength and bear more nourishing transformative fruit. But we need to be vigilant, for the greatest and most dangerous of all the challenges we each face is our own ego. And that is the one obstacle that can take us down and destroy our achievements.

When we speak of the need for transformative leadership in today's world, present the elements of the conceptual framework to others, and engage in the process of developing leadership capabilities, it is important to guard against the error of thinking that we have become transformed leaders. With deep humility, we need to recognize how far we have to go in order to truly exemplify in our lives the transformative leadership that society requires. This kind of leadership is an ideal that guides our actions; however, there is always more to learn and plenty of room to improve.

This creates a strange paradox. On the one hand, this book has the purpose of encouraging the practice of transformative leadership in society. On the other, one of the main obstacles to exercising true transformative leadership is *ambition* for a position of leadership. This is one of the more important flaws in the prevailing mental models of leadership described in Chapter III. When we analyze more deeply the origin of this ambition, we see that it is closely related to the mental model of competition within an adversarial culture, which cultivates the love of power.

Some will argue that ambition is a positive quality that is necessary for progress. However, upon analysis, we can recognize that ambition in itself is neither good nor bad. It is a tool that can be used to do good or to do harm. If we have the ambition to develop greater knowledge, virtue or capability in order to better serve, we are using our ambition well. However, if we desire to stand out from others, motivated by a craving for self-aggrandizement and the desire to glorify our own abilities and achievements, we succumb to egotistic ambition — a trap that inevitably leads to disunity and conflict. But the question is even more complex. Even egotistic ambition can serve as a motivating force that leads to action, hard work and progress. In this sense, it can play a positive role in the first stages of maturation; but soon this type of ambition reaches its limits.

Those motivated by egotistic ambition promote themselves, call attention to what they have done and act based on personal interest. If they are not able to move past this type of ambition and commit themselves to values and ideals that create unselfish motivation, egotistic ambition will slowly destroy both the group with which they work and themselves. This type of ambition disguises the desire for domination. As a result, the actions of an egotistic leader tend to awaken a spirit of competition in the group that leads to power struggles.

TO WHAT ARE YOU FAITHFUL?[2]

In the play, A Man for All Seasons, Richard Rich admired (Thomas) More's honesty and integrity and wanted to be employed by him. He pleaded, "Employ me."

More answered, "No."

Again Rich pleaded, "Employ me!" and again the answer was no.

Then Rich made this pitiful yet endearing promise: "I would be steadfast!"

Sir Thomas, knowing what mastered Richard Rich, answered, "Richard, you couldn't answer for yourself even so far as tonight," meaning, "You might profess to be faithful now, but all it will take is a different circumstance, the right bribe or pressure, and you will be so controlled by your ambition and pride that you would not be faithful to me."

Sir Thomas More's prognosis came to pass that very night, for Richard Rich betrayed him!

▶ EGO

According to myth, Lucifer was the angel with the highest rank in heaven. Although he was already at the top, he was not content to serve God. He wanted to be as powerful as God. When he was unable to achieve this egotistic ambition, he chose to become the lord of hell and to compete with God. When people allow their egos to dominate them, we cannot trust them to be faithful to anyone except themselves.

When ideals of service become confused with personal interest, or even worse, when personal interest trumps the spirit of service in making decisions or taking action, leadership becomes corrupt. Any seemingly 'good' action is then tainted. Those who witness in their leaders the desire for self-glorification will be suspicious and distrustful. Without trust, collaboration is impossible, as it requires a foundation of trust and mutual respect.

▶ AMBITION TO SERVE

In contrast, those who strive to practice transformative leadership consciously endeavor to subdue their egocentric tendencies. Their ambition is focused on bettering their capabilities to love, to serve, to work together for the common good and to contribute in the construction of a more just, united, and peaceful world. This type of ambition creates passion and motivates greater effort than that generated by egotistic ambition. Furthermore, selfless ambition motivated by a spirit of service inspires greater self-sacrifice and more valuable contributions to collective transformation than egotistic ambition could ever achieve. Moreover, the effect of selfless ambition on others is completely different from the effect of egotistic ambition. Since those motivated by selfless ambition sincerely desire the well-being of all, they make decisions and act as disinterestedly as possible to promote the common good. Such noble conduct tends to inspire in others similar efforts.

▶ QUALITIES THAT PROTECT US

Although we have thoroughly explored the ideal that we seek, we also recognize that egocentric tendencies are part of human nature from which we can never completely liberate ourselves. However, we can consciously oppose these tendencies, cultivating those qualities that serve as antidotes, such as: *modesty, detachment, fair-mindedness* and *purity of intention*. True modesty, no matter how great our capabilities, is born from the recognition of our multiple defects, limitations and errors, when compared to the lofty ideals to which all great spiritual leaders throughout history have beckoned humanity. The consciousness of these weaknesses impels us to an awareness of the subtle manifestations of ego and how it can entrap us in self-serving agendas. We can transcend this trap by focusing on our higher purpose, seeking to become pure channels through which inspired actions flow.

Modesty opens the path to the practice of *detachment*. When we are aware that we have only a partial perception of truth, we become open to different points of view and try to understand how these complement our own understanding. When we recognize that we have limitations and are subject to error, we can consider any suggestion, modification, or even criticism of our ideas and actions, without becoming defensive.

Fair-mindedness is closely related to the moral responsibility of applying in all our actions the truths we have recognized. Acting with fair-mindedness implies that we do not allow our personal interests to interfere with what we know to be true in a given situation. This helps us to develop and exercise willpower — a necessary intermediate step between knowledge and action. It protects us from the danger of pretending to uphold a loftier standard than we are willing to live by.

Modesty, detachment and fair-mindedness are prerequisites for *purity of intention*. When our actions are motivated by fear of punishment or the hope of reward, or when we consciously seek our own advantage, we lack purity of intention. In comparison, acts of service motivated by love reflect purity of intention in its loftiest form. Love, which engenders the desire to serve others and to consider their needs before our own, is the best antidote to the poison of self-aggrandizing ambition.

The greater our capabilities, the more vigilant we must be to oppose our egocentric tendencies. Our knowledge, wealth, or position can create within us feelings of superiority and the belief that we are more worthy than others. Therefore, the more capabilities we acquire, the more deeply we need to develop the qualities of modesty, detachment, fair-mindedness and purity of intention through daily practice and self-evaluation.

In our pursuit of transformative leadership, we are aspiring to a very high standard requiring a lifetime commitment as individuals. We are fortunate to have had inspiring examples of leadership in our recent history - individuals such as Mahatma Gandhi, Mother Teresa, Martin Luther King, and Nelson Mandela. However, at this critical time of accelerating crises, we do not have the luxury of waiting for selfless charismatic leaders to arise and point the way to a better future. The needs of our age require that we each take up the challenge in our own spheres of influence and become those individuals who will commit to "being" the change the future demands of us, with the full recognition that pursuit of power and self-interest will only perpetuate the tyranny of the past. It is an arduous journey we cannot afford to ignore.

How the future unfolds is hard to predict. However, it is undeniable that significant world-encompassing change is inevitable. We can facilitate the required transformation by becoming willing instruments for a better future, learning the path as we collaborate together.

REFERENCES AND NOTES

FRONT MATERIALS

1. 'Abdu'l-Bahá, *Secret of Divine Civilization,* Baha'i Publishing Trust, Wilmette, 1970, pp. 34-40.

2. Books authored or co-authored by Ms. Hernandez can be found at www.gemas.discernir.com.

3. Universal House of Justice, *Tribute to Dr. Eloy Anello*, October 6, 2009.

INTRODUCTION

1. Mezirow, Jack & Associates. *Learning as Transformation,* Jossey Bass; John Wiley and Sons, 2000.

CHAPTER I: CRISIS OF OUR TIMES

1. Covey, Stephen R. *Principle-Centered Leadership*, Simon & Schuster, New York, 1990, p. 19.

2. Universal House of Justice. *Second Message to World Congress*, November 26, 1992.

3. Shoghi Effendi, quoted by the Universal House of Justice. *The Promise of World Peace*, 1986, p. 2

4. Freire, Paolo. *Education for Critical Consciousness,* Seabury Press, New York, 1973, p. 7.

5. Peter Senge popularized the term, "mental model," in his book, *The Fifth Discipline*, but it was originally coined by Kenneth Craik in his 1943 book*, The Nature of Explanation.*

6. Kuhn, Thomas. *The Structure of Scientific Revolutions*, 1962.

7. Sheldrake, Rupert. *The Science Delusion: Freeing the Spirit of Enquiry*, Coronet, Great Britain, 2012.

8. J. S. Bell. *On the Einstein–Poldolsky–Rosen Paradox*, Physics **1** 195-200 (1964). This provided proof for the *EPR Paradox*, a thought experiment elaborated in 1935 by Einstein, Rosen and Podolsky as a critique of quantum mechanics.

9. Field, C.B. et al. *Managing the Risks of Extreme Events and Disasters to Advance Climate Change Adaptation*, Special Report of the Intergovernmental Panel on Climate Change, Cambridge University press, June 2012.

10. Lovelock, James. *The Vanishing Face of Gaia*, Basic Books, 2009.

11. Lovelock, James. "Hands Up for the Gaia Hypothesis," *Nature*, 344 (6262), 1990, pp. 100-102.

12. Sahtouris, Elisabet. "Prologue to a New Model of a Living Universe," *Mind Before Matter: Vision of a New Science of Consciousness,* edited by Trish Pfeiffer, John E. Mack, Paul Devereux, 2007.

13. Capra, Fritjof. *The Tao of Physics*, Bantam Books, New York, 1977, p. 298.

14. *Conference on World Financial and Economic Crisis*, "Wide-ranging proposals to mitigate world financial crisis adopted by consensus at United Nations Conference in New York," 26 June 2009.

15. Gadonneix, Pierre. President of World Energy Council, Address to the Executive Assembly, Reykjavik, 2009.

16. Arnold Toynbee, quoted by Sorokin, Pitirim A. *The Social Philosophies of Our Epoch of Crisis*. Editorial Aguilar: Madrid, 1960, pp. 158-159.

17. Rogers, Everett M. *Diffusion of Innovations*, New York, NY. Simon & Schuster, 2003.

18. Keyes, Ken. *The Hundredth Monkey*, Camarillo: DeVorss & Co., 1984.

19. Sheldrake, Rupert. *Morphic Resonance: the Nature of Formative Causation*, Park Street Press, Rochester, Vermont, Toronto, Canada, 2009.

20. de Mello, Anthony. *The Prayer of the Frog*, Gujarat Sahitya Pakash, Anand, India, 1989, Vol. 2, p. 202.

21. World Health Organization. *Report on Technical Discussions: Recommendations and Main Conclusions*, Forty-first Assembly on World Health, Geneva, May 1988, p. 7.

CHAPTER II: MENTAL MODELS OF HUMAN NATURE AND SOCIETY

1. Sahtouris, Elisabet. *Gaia: The Human Journey From Chaos to Cosmos,* New York, Pocket Books, 1989, pp. 207-208.

2. McGregor, Douglas quoted by Fred Luthans in *Organizational Behavior*. New York: McGraw Hill, 1977, p. 20.

3. Ibid.

4. Montagu, Ashley. *Darwin, Competition and Cooperation*, Reprinted,Westport, Connecticut, Greenwood Press, 1973, p. 72.

5. UNESCO. *Seville Statement on Violence*, originally written and signed by 20 Nobel prize winners for the International Year of Peace in Seville, Spain, May 16, 1988, officially adopted in 1989 by UNESCO.

6. Ibid.

7. Definition by the *National Institute of General Medical Sciences* of the National Institutes of Health, http://publications.nigms. nih. gov/thenewgenetics/glossary.html

8. Sheldrake, Rupert. *The Presence of the Past: Morphic Resonance and the Memory of Nature*, Park Street Press, Rochester, Vermont, Toronto, Canada, 2012.

9. Nwachuku, A. *Critiquing Economic Frameworks in Sustainable Development: Health Equity, Resource Management and Materialism*, Columbia University PhD Thesis, 2011.

10. Knafo, A., C. Zahn-Waxler, C. Van Hulle, J. L. Robinson, and S. H. Rhee. "The developmental origins of a disposition toward empathy: Genetic and environmental contributions." *Emotion,* 2008, 8: 737-752.

11. Eisenberg, N., I. K. Guthrie, B. C. Murphy, S. A. Shepard, A. Cumberland, and G. Carlo. "Consistency and development of prosocial dispositions: A longitudinal study," *Child Development,* 1999, 70: 1360-1372.

12. Preston, S. D., and F B. M. de Waal. "Empathy: Its ultimate and proximate bases." *Behavioral and Brain Sciences,* 2002, 25: 1-72.

13. Karlberg, Michael. *Beyond the Culture of Contest – From Adversarialism to Mutualism in an Age of Interdependence*, Oxford. George Ronald Publisher, 2004.

14. Davies, James B et al. "The World Distribution of Household Wealth," *United Nations University, World Institute for Development Economics Research*, Feb 2008.

15. Kohn, Alfie. *No Contest: The Case Against Competition*. Boston: Houghton Mifflin, 1986/1992, Chapter 3.

16. Ibid, pp. 59-60, 206, 217-20, 225-26, 236, 242.

CHAPTER III: DOMINANT MODELS OF LEADERSHIP

1. de Mello, Anthony. *The Prayer of the Frog*, Gujarat Sahitya Pakash, Anand, India, 1989, Vol. 1, p. 117.

2. Account of a personal experience by Eloy Anello.

3. Bahá'í International Community. *The Prosperity of Humankind*, Haifa, Israel, 1995, p. 20.

CHAPTER IV: A CONCEPTUAL FRAMEWORK OF TRANSFORMATIVE
LEADERSHIP

1. Parliament of the World's Religions. *Declaration Toward a Global Ethic*, 4 September 1993, Chicago, USA.

2. Hemingway, Ernest. quoted by Sue Johnson. *Hold Me Tight*, Little, Brown and Company, New York, 2008, p. 255.

3. Polelle, Mark Robert. *Leadership: Fifty Great Leaders and the Worlds They Made*, Greenwood Press: Westport, CT, 2008, p.xiv.

4. de Mello, Anthony. *The Prayer of the Frog*, Vol. II, Anand, India, 1989, p. 193.

5. 'Abdu'l-Bahá. *The Secret of Divine Civilization*, p.2, Ocean database, http://bahai-education.org/ocean.

6. Universal House of Justice. *The Promise of World Peace*, Bahá'í World Center, 1985, p. 2.

7. Bohm, David. *Wholeness and the Implicate Order*, Ark Paperbacks, London and New York, 1983, p. 8.

8. Senge, Peter. *The Fifth Discipline*, Currency Doubleday, New York, 2006.

9. Covey, Stephen. *Principle-Centered Leadership*, Simon & Schuster, New York p.18.

10. de Mello, Anthony. *The Prayer of the Frog,* Vol. I, Anand, India, 1989, p. 38.

11. Lample, Paul. *Revelation and Social Reality*, Palabra Publications, West Palm Beach, Florida, 2009, p. 173.

12. Yang Ming-che. *Principle or mind?* (originally published 1969), Ministry of Foreign Affairs, Republic of China (Taiwan), 2013, http://taiwantoday.tw/ct.asp?xItem=140526&CtNode=124.

13. Rogers, Carl. *Client-Centered Therapy: Its Current Practice, Implications and Theory,* London: Constable, 1951.

14. Wiles, Nicola, et al. "Cognitive behavioural therapy as an adjunct to pharmacotherapy for primary care based patients with treatment resistant depression: results of the CoBalT randomized controlled trial," published online *www.thelancet.com,* December 7, 2012.

15. Proverbs 29:18. *Holy Bible*, Old Testament.

16. Gardner, John. *On Leadership*, Free Press, New York, 1993, p. xi.

17. Russell, Peter. *The Global Brain*, J.P. Tarcher, Inc.: Los Angeles, 1983, p. 130.

18. Covey, Stephen. *Principle-Centered Leadership*, Simon & Schuster, New York, p. 34.

19. 'Abdu'l-Bahá. *The Promulgation of Universal Peace*, Wilmette: Baha'i Publishing Trust, 1982, p. 157.

CHAPTER V: CAPABILITIES FOR PERSONAL TRANSFORMATION

1. Senge, Peter, et. al. *Presence: Human Purpose and the Field of the Future*, Doubleday, New York, 2004.

2. Mezirow, Jack & Associates. *Learning as Transformation*, Jossey Bass; John Wiley and Sons, 2000.

3. Scharmer, C. Otto. *Theory U: Leading from the Future as it Emerges*, Society for Organizational Learning: Cambridge, MA, 2007.

4. Senge, Peter, et. al. *The Fifth Discipline Fieldbook*, New York, Doubleday, 1994, p. 243.

5. Senge, Peter, *The Fifth Discipline*, Currency Doubleday, New York, 2006, p. 93.

6. Senge, Peter, *The Fifth Discipline*, Currency Doubleday, New York, 2006, pp. 103-110.

7. Senge, Peter, *The Fifth Discipline*, Currency Doubleday, New York, 2006, pp. 94-103.

8. Gleick, James. *Chaos: Making a New Science*, Viking Penguin, 1987.

9. Prigogine, Ilya and Isabelle Stengers. *Order Out Of Chaos: Man's New Dialogue With Nature,* Flamingo, 1984.

10. Capra, Fritjof. *The Hidden Connections: A Science for Sustainable Living*, Anchor Books, New York, 2002, p. 14.

11. Covey, Stephen R. *Principle-Centered Leadership*, Simon & Schuster, New York, 1990, p. 38.

CHAPTER VI: CAPABILITIES FOR TRANSFORMATION OF INTERPERSONAL RELATIONSHIPS

1. Fromm, Erich. *The Art of Loving*, Harper and Row, 1956, p. 24.

2. Hofman, David quoting 'Abdu'l-Bahá. *The Renewal of Civilization*, George Ronald, London, 1972, p. 62.

3. Bahá'u'lláh, quoted in *Consultation: A Compilation*, Bahá'í Publishing Trust, Wilmette, IL, 1980, p. 3.

4. Gardner, John. *Multiple Intelligences: The Theory in Practice,* BasicBooks, Harper Collins Publishers, Inc., New York, 1993.

5. *Prosperity of Humankind*, Bahá'í International Community, Section 3, 1995.

CHAPTER VII: CAPABILITIES FOR SOCIAL TRANSFORMATION

1. Karlberg, Michael. *Beyond the Culture of Contest: From Adversarialism to Mutualism in an Age of Interdependence*, George Ronald Publisher, Oxford, 2004, pp. 28-30.

2. Attributed to Lewis Carroll. (English mathematician and novelist, especially known for *Alice's Adventures in Wonderland*. 1832-1898).

3. UN Global Compact website: http://www.unglobalcompact.org/aboutthegc/thetenprinciples/index.html.

4. Petersmann, Ernst-Ulrich. "Time for a United Nations 'Global Compact' for Integrating Human Rights into the Law of Worldwide Organizations: Lessons from European Integration," *European Journal of International Law*, Vol. 13 No. 3, 621-650, 2002.

5. Blanchard, Ken and Paul Hersey. *Management of Organizational Behavior*, Prentice Hall, Inc., New Jersey, 1982, pp. 160- 161.

6. Toynbee, Arnold J. *A Study of History*. Abridgement by D.C. Somervell, Oxford University Press, Oxford, December 1987.

7. Shoghi Effendi. *Promised Day is Come*, Bahá'í Publishing Trust, Wilmette, 1943.

8. Sahtouris, Elisabeth. *Gaia: The Human Journey From Chaos to Cosmos,* New York, Pocket Books, 1989.

9. American anthropologist, 1901-1978.

CHAPTER VIII: INTEGRATING CAPABILITIES

1. Universal House of Justice. *The Promise of World Peace,* Bahá'í World Center, Haifa, Israel, 1985.

EPILOGUE: A WORD ABOUT AMBITION

1. de Mello, Anthony. *The Prayer of the Frog*, Gujarat Sahitya Pa-kash, Anand, India, 1989, Vol. 1, p. 91.

2. Covey, Stephen R. *Principle-Centered Leadership*, Simon & Schuster, New York, 1990, p. 55.

INDEX

and transformative learning 7–9
existential 22
financial 29
of our times 5, 17–33, 31, 117
of values 33–34
critical mass 11, 32

D

Darwin, Charles 40–41
Declaration Toward a Global Ethic
    83, 100
de Mello, Anthony 101
democracy
    adversarial 72, 77, 78
    participatory 72–73, 78
    problems with 74–78
    representative 72, 76–77
determination 131, 150, 153, 158
diversity 43, 169, 186
    and collaboration 188–189
    and consultation 169
    of views 146, 167–168
    unity in 173–177, 185–186, 208,
        210
domination 69, 93, 183
    and ambition 215
    and power 183
    in the family 208
    leadership by 70, 86
    mental model of 185–188

E

education 101, 154, 167, 194
    adult 3, 12
    and social justice 180
    continuing 201
    empowering 137, 186, 189–194
    shared vision 195–197
    universal 30
ego 90, 163, 214
    and ambition 214, 216–217, 218
    and self-evaluation 128, 129
    and transcendence 113
Einstein, Albert 115

elections 75, 78, 79
    with candidates 75
    without candidates 75
empathy 10, 45, 109, 155
    and listening 119, 161, 172
encouragement 67, 156, 162–163
    and abundance 164–165
    and acceptance 163
    and mutual empowerment 184
    in the family 210–211
    self 165–166
epigenetics 43
equality
    and justice 179
    and power 183
    between the sexes 208
ethical principles 35, 191
    and conceptual framework 9–11,
        138
    and corporate social responsibil-
        ity 198
    and mental models 136–137
    and rectitude of conduct 155,
        157
    and transformation 100
    and transformative leadership 79
    and truth 102
    and unity in diversity 177
ethics 10, 24, 35, 41
evidence 9, 10, 19, 20, 21, 23, 29,
        35, 38, 45, 79, 136, 138, 181
    -based xiv, 40
    scientific 9, 25, 40, 42, 98, 102,
        138, 191
experience 45, 53, 66, 67, 73,
        98–100, 111, 124, 184
    and collaborative relationships
        188
    and learning cycle 131–132
    and self-discipline 154
    and self-encouragement 166
    and self-evaluation 130
    and the learning cycle 191–192
    and transcendence 112

Mother Teresa 219

N

nobility 10, 59, 154
  and abundance 165
  and encouragement 162–163
  essential 49, 92, 108–112, 121

O

oneness
  and collaboration 188
  and racism 55
  new paradigm of 25, 26
  of humanity 30, 170

P

paradigm 59
  definition 2
  new 29, 38, 188
  shift 20–27, 53
Parliament of the World's Religions 83, 100
perseverance 70, 79
  and creative initiative 149
  capability of 151–153
population 27, 208
power 9, 11, 51, 69, 78, 86, 158
  as capacity 182–184
  love of 75, 215
  of decision-making 76, 85
  of encouragement 210
  of love 161
  of mental models 38
  over 155
  struggle 56, 62, 77, 215
  to act 12, 200
  transcendent 165
  use of 185
prejudice
  and consultation 171
  and disintegration 28
  and justice 180
  and mental models 6

and personal transformation 93
and racism 54
and truth 102
and unity 177
psychology 45
  developmental 167
  humanistic 109
  positive 109

R

racism 54–55
rectitude of conduct 155–158
  in the family 209
reflection 99, 181
  and learning cycle 123, 191–192
  and truth 105–106
  individual 96
  on action 12, 79, 131–139, 209
  self 193
religion 202
  and global ethic 83
  and historical perspective 202
  and ideal truth 100
  and mental model 137
  and unity in diversity 174
root causes 103, 156, 186
Russell, Peter 115

S

scarcity 52–53, 164
Scharmer, Otto 134
self-discipline 108, 112
  capability of 153–155
self-evaluation 79, 219
self-interest 24, 128, 140
  and love 161
  and self-evaluation 128
  mental model 45, 53
Seligman, Martin 109
Senge, Peter 21, 97, 133, 135, 143, 145
service 54–55, 162, 195
  and ambition 217
  and capabilities 117

and leadership 84–90
and love 162, 218
and reciprocity 186
and self-encouragement 166
and self-evaluation 127, 131
and transcendence 112–113
in the family 210
spirit of 75–76, 79, 155, 171, 217
to the common good 10, 35, 184
Seville Statement on Violence 42
shared vision 69, 95, 115, 173
  capability of elaborating
    194–198
Sheldrake, Rupert 22, 32
Shoghi Effendi 204
slavery 55, 57, 63
  abolition of 53
social evolution 174, 204–205
society 17, 77, 79, 99, 112, 139,
    208, 214
  and human nobility 108
  and moral leadership 5
  and rise of civilization 204
  and social evolution 204–205
  and the family 208–209
  and transformation 92–96
  and transformative leadership
    117
  and truth 106
  crisis in 18–33
  disunity in 19
  division 174
  global 100, 114, 204
  just 180
  leadership 64, 81
  mental model 7–11, 38–40,
    50–59
  mental models 191
  mutualistic 184–188
  problems 116
  vision for 115
Spencer, Herbert 41
spiritual 86, 92
  disease 57

heritage 11, 19, 83
laws 105
leaders 157, 218
principles 99
teachings 109
truth 106, 110
values 10
well-being 25
suffrage 53
systemic thinking 140–151

T

The Declaration of Human
    Rights 100
Theory U 134
tipping point 32
Toynbee, Arnold 31, 203
transcendence 10, 84
  capability of 112–116
transformation 71, 82
  and learning 8–12
  and nobility 109, 111
  and service 89–90
  and transcendence 112
  and truth 96–97, 99
  interpersonal 159–178
  learning process 123
  of leadership 30
  personal 44, 82, 103, 127–157
  personal and social 31–32, 35,
    58–59, 91–96, 121–122,
    123
  social 105, 111–112, 179–205
  truth 100
Truman, Harry 90
trustworthiness 19, 84, 116, 119,
    129, 157
truth 119, 137–139, 146, 218
  and consultation 166–176
  and justice 181
  and learning 133–134
  investigation and application
    121
  search for 140, 157

U